THE BLACK
MALE
HANDBOOK

Also by Kevin Powell

No Sleep Till Brooklyn: New and Selected Poems

Someday We'll All Be Free

Who Shot Ya? Three Decades of Hiphop Photography

*Who's Gonna Take the Weight? Manhood, Race,
and Power in America*

Step into a World: A Global Anthology of the New Black Literature

Keepin' It Real: Post-MTV Reflections on Race, Sex, and Politics

recognize: Poems

In the Tradition: An Anthology of Young Black Writers

THE BLACK
MALE
HANDBOOK

A BLUEPRINT FOR LIFE

EDITED BY

KEVIN POWELL

FOREWORD BY

HILL HARPER

ATRIA BOOKS
New York   London   Toronto   Sydney

ATRIA BOOKS

A Division of Simon & Schuster, Inc.
1230 Avenue of the Americas
New York, NY 10020

First Atria Books trade paperback edition September 2008

ATRIA BOOKS and colophon are trademarks of Simon & Schuster, Inc.

For information about special discounts for bulk purchases,
please contact Simon & Schuster Special Sales at 1-800-456-6798 or
business@simonand schuster.com

Designed by Davina Mock-Maniscalco

Manufactured in the United States of America

1   3   5   7   9   10   8   6   4   2

Library of Congress Cataloging-in-Publication Data

The Black male handbook: a blueprint for life / edited by Kevin Powell;
foreword by Hill Harper.
p.   cm.
Includes bibliographical references.
1. African American men—Handbooks, manuals, etc.   2. African American
men—Social conditions.   3. African American men—Conduct of life.
4. Masculinity—United States.   I. Powell, Kevin.
E185.86.B52566   2008
305.38'896073—dc22   20008023403

ISBN-13: 978–1–4165–9224–2
ISBN-10:   1–4165–9224–5

For us Black men and us Black boys

He who asks questions, cannot avoid the answers.
—African proverb, from Cameroon

One thing they cannot prohibit—
   The strong men . . . coming on
—Sterling Brown, "Strong Men"

Nobody can give you equality or justice or anything.
If you're a man, you take it.
—Malcolm X, speaking in Harlem, New York,
December 20, 1964

Don't grieve for me my art remains
like a dart from the speaker to your heart
—Jay-Z, "Lucky Me"

Contents

Contents

Foreword

By Hill Harper

*I believe that unarmed truth and unconditional love will have
the final word.*

—Dr. Martin Luther King, Jr.

*And so we must straighten our backs and work for our free-
dom. A man can't ride you unless your back is bent.*

—Dr. Martin Luther King, Jr.

These two commanding quotes spoke to what Dr. King had
hoped the future would hold for all Americans, especially
Black men. However, it seems as if "brotherhood," "unconditional
love," and "truth" are not as prevalent in our society as he once
believed they could and would be. Forty years after Dr. King's
death, struggle remains the most widespread practice in most of
our communities. We cannot allow this to be our legacy—we
must begin to rewrite our history, starting right now.

The story thus far is somewhat alarming. When one out of
every fifteen African American men over the age of eighteen is in
prison, we are clearly in crisis mode. But that's not the worst of
it—between the ages of twenty and thirty-four, fully one in nine
Black men are behind bars. Include those on parole, probation, or
otherwise involved in the criminal justice system, and that number jumps to one in three. That Wynton Marsalis album title,
From the Plantation to the Penitentiary, is real. The prison-

industrial complex is alive and well. Moreover, many of our young men who are *not* in trouble with the law feel stuck, as if they can't get ahead. It's imperative that we all become aware of our options outside a system that doesn't appear to believe in the strength and promise of Black men.

Instead, many of our Black men are lost—looking for inspiration, motivation, and guidance. Like the narrator of Ralph Ellison's 1952 classic *Invisible Man*, we are silently and sometimes invisibly searching, crying, and yearning to be heard and understood in a world that seems to ignore us. Unless, of course, we happen to be a "baller" who can "make it rain," "rock tha mic," or "push a Bentley."

As Black men, we must encourage one another to take back our hearts and minds by recharging our mental, cultural, and spiritual beings. Only then can we overcome our culture of fear. Fear is **F**alse **E**vidence **A**ppearing **R**eal. We've been systematically taught to be afraid of our true greatness, our true potential. Don't let other people project their fears on you. I believe that the biggest civil rights challenge facing us as Black men in this culture is that of self-esteem and self-worth. *The Black Male Handbook* addresses this issue head-on.

As I wrote in my book *Letters to a Young Brother: MANifest Your Destiny*, I don't want my brothers simply to be happy. I want all of you to be *unreasonably* happy. By this I mean happier than anybody expects you to be—even yourself. Which is exactly why I recommend that you read this handbook. The depth and intelligence presented in the pages that follow represent a road map to your life's journey, and more than that, to the priceless realization of how magnificent it is meant to be. The magnificence of your journey will not be measured by how many cars, girls, or Jordans you acquire. Instead, the measure of your magnificence will depend on whether you do like your ancestors and add more to this world than you take away. Simply put: Are you a giver or a taker? A lover or a hater? A boy or a man?

In the studio, listening to tracks from his latest album, Usher recently reminded me of this passage from 1 Corinthians 13:11:

> When I was a child, I talked like a child, I thought like a child, I reasoned like a child. When I became a man, I put childish ways behind me.

This passage serves as a reminder for all of us to take stock of our own manhood. And I believe that *The Black Male Handbook* can serve a similar purpose in our lives. Brother Kevin Powell has assembled an amazing group of brilliant Black men for this book, such as Lasana Hotep writing about how "Spirituality is the manifestation of this divine connection in one's daily life." Or Jeff Johnson telling us, "We've got to blow up the mind-set that we are competing against one another to do things that in many cases we need to be working together to do." Or Ryan Mack asking us, "Why are some of us more concerned with material wealth than with establishing trust funds for our children?"

The Black Male Handbook must be read thoughtfully and carefully. Use this book as I like to use all books; as an interactive tool. Underline passages that resonate with you. Write your own ideas in the margins. This book is no different than a hammer or a nail—use it as a tool to aid you in building the life you want. In order to become the architects of our own lives, we must create a blueprint. A plan. Most architects, when designing their structure, use a pencil for their blueprints. Why do they use a pencil? So they can erase and make modifications. None of us are perfect, but we are here for divine reasons—so there are no mistakes to erase. But we may need to make modifications as we move forward into our future.

Foreword

I'm from the entertainment business, and I believe that my industry has done more to decimate the self-esteem of young brothers in the last ten years than any other industry. That's why I'm making it my business to tell you that your manhood is not measured by the size of the rims on your car or the size of the Rolex on your wrist. Even if you don't have flashy material possessions, you can create the exact destiny that you want. You can and will win at your life and be unreasonably happy. This world, this universe, will conspire to help you win. Please believe that there is nothing you cannot do. Remember, you are the architect of your life. The possibilities are limitless. You are magnificent. You are brilliant. You are already wealthy beyond measure. You don't ever have to quit—because there is nothing you can't do. You can take risks relentlessly to create the life you design. The only thing that will limit you is the capacity of your imagination.

Do I agree with everything that every author says in this book? No. And if *you* don't agree with some of the things, that's okay. In fact, it's great. That simply means you are a critical thinker who doesn't accept everything you read at face value. Think about what the authors in this book have to say, and decide for yourself whether you agree with their ideas. The authors represent many different points of view, but they share the same goal: to uplift the lives of Black males and help us work together to build stronger communities. Use the words on these pages to stimulate your own thoughts about the way you would like to live your life.

Reading this book reminded me of the time I traveled to Kenya and saw the Maasai warriors. And interestingly enough, when these strong, proud Black men went out into the bush to hunt, they held hands. Did it seem odd or effeminate to me? Not at all. Instead, it represented a deep-seated brotherly affection, mutual support, and confidence in their self-worth as men. Like the Maasai I saw in Kenya, I feel comfortable being able to look a brother in the eye and say "I love you, brother." And so I say, to whatever brother is reading these words right now, know that I love you. I want what is best for you. Recognize how magnificent you already are! Like your history, your destiny is majestic! It is up to you to manifest it. My brothers, you all personify greatness. You *will* win at your life, if you choose to do so. You *will* be *unreasonably* happy. So *Dream it. Believe it. See it.* Now do it. Let's not just enjoy *The Black Male Handbook*. Let's all put its wisdom to use.

Editor's Note

The seeds for *The Black Male Handbook* were planted over twenty years ago when I was a teenage college student at Rutgers University in New Brunswick, New Jersey. I had grown up fatherless, reared by a poor young Black woman in Jersey City. My concept of manhood, of Black manhood specifically, had been shaped by that absent dad and the destructive images I saw all about me: street hustlers, thieves, pimps, numbers runners, drug dealers, and bootleg preachers who seemed to have more interest in our meager earnings than our souls. Add to that the parade of backward Black male media images in the form of sitcoms, the Black characters on *The Little Rascals*, and elsewhere, and my self-esteem and self-worth were shot right from the beginning of my life. But that changed when I got to Rutgers, *not* because of what I was taught in the classrooms of that school, but because of what I learned outside them. In the E185 section of the Alexander Library on College Avenue, where I worked for over two years, I discovered Black males who I hadn't previously known existed— like Malcolm X, George Jackson, Frederick Douglass, Nat Turner,

Editor's Note

Benjamin Banneker, and Paul Robeson, who had attended Rutgers two generations before I did.

Additionally, two Black male leaders of the 1980s would have a consciousness-shifting effect on how I viewed Black manhood and, by extension, myself: the Reverend Jesse Jackson, because of his two historic runs for president in 1984 and 1988. And Minister Louis Farrakhan, because of his controversial and outspoken leadership of the Nation of Islam, including its national resurrection during that decade. All these years later, I am my own man and no longer follow either Jackson or Farrakhan. But back then, as a wild-eyed and intellectually hungry young Black male, both blew my mind.

They blew my mind because it was the first time I'd ever witnessed Black males who spoke the way they did, who moved people to action as they did, who seemed, at least on the surface, to be positive alternatives to the Black male voices and images I had become accustomed to. Not only did I become a registered voter, a student leader, and an activist because of Reverend Jackson's campaigns, but for the first time in my life as a Black male, I believed anything was possible. "Run Jesse Run" and "I am somebody" may sound mad corny and clichéd in the twenty-first century, but in the crack era of the 1980s it was liberating.

Likewise with Minister Farrakhan and the Nation of Islam. When I went to hear him speak at Madison Square Garden in the fall of 1984, it was completely sold out. My college buddies and I, also Black males, literally stood for three hours listening to a speech of which I cannot recall one single line today. No matter—what I do recall is the image of what seemed like thousands of well-groomed, clean-cut, and immaculately suited young Black males whose speech, posture, and demeanor illuminated a kind of discipline and sense of purpose I had never seen in my life. Although I am a Christian today, I spent several years as a Muslim, first with the Nation of Islam and later as what we call an orthodox Muslim. And the Islamic experience was certainly the beginning of my changing my diet ("do not eat pork, brothers, ever . . ." went the refrain) and my lifestyle.

I would be remiss if I did not add that the 1980s was really the beginning of a downward spiral for Black males in America, a spiral we are still in the throes of today, in forms and shapes that seem worse than ever. Again, it was the era of crack cocaine decimating our inner-city communities nationwide. Crack did one of three things to Black males: It turned many of us into coldhearted drug dealers who would get rich or die trying. It turned many of us into "crackheads" or "baseheads," long-suffering addicts who would trade in our own families for the next high. And it put large numbers of us in prisons nationwide. I strongly believe, now, that my four years at Rutgers are what saved me from a similar fate.

At Rutgers I was a leader of an organization called 100 Black Men of Rutgers University, where our very basic goal was to have 100 Black males graduate from Rutgers College, one of RU's many schools, in the same academic year. As we actively supported one another's efforts to graduate, 100 Black Men grew into *the* organization on campus. Sadly, in spite of being one of the leaders, I never graduated myself. We held weekly meetings that were part "safe spaces" and part counseling sessions for Black male students. Taking it a step further, we actively engaged in mentoring younger Black male students, and we even created a high school recruitment weekend to encourage Black males to attend Rutgers.

Through much of the 1990s, my life was transformed by being on the first season of MTV's *The Real World,* and by writing cover stories for Quincy Jones's *Vibe* magazine, many of them about the late Tupac Shakur. For sure, hiphop both saved and changed my life, on so many levels: I have been deeply immersed in hiphop since I was a preteen—as a b-boy and graffiti writer back in the day; as a hiphop journalist and curator of the very first exhibit on hiphop history at the Rock and Roll Hall of Fame; as someone who, today, routinely uses hiphop as a tool for social change in my community work with young people nationwide. So, as a Black male, it has been profound and deeply traumatizing to watch the deterioration of hiphop music beginning in the mid-1990s, all for the sake of profit; to be there in Las Vegas when Tupac's death was announced; to be doubly shaken when, less than a year later, the Notorious B.I.G. was also mysteriously murdered. And the debates about the death of hiphop have carried into the new millennium as this once genius music, fueled by Black and Latino inner-city males, has become a caricature of its former self.

And over this same time period there have been numerous public forums, reports, and studies on the state of Black males. These studies and conversations have continued into the new millennium. Frustrated by the fact that most of them continually talked about the crises and problems confronting Black males while offering little or no practical solutions, a small group of organizers and I launched a ten-city State of Black Men tour in 2004. Our purpose was multidimensional: 1) to confirm that the challenges confronting Black males are indeed national in scope; 2) to begin to identify younger Black males who had actually created models of success in our communities; and 3) to shift the leadership of the conversations about Black males away from the civil rights generation to those of us born on the heels of, or in the aftermath of, the civil rights era, to those of us weaned on the explosion of the mass-media culture, the technology revolution, and, yes, hiphop.

We spent the next few years localizing our work in New York City. That work included regular town-hall meetings, mentoring sessions, workshops at schools, foster care programs, and prisons, and a three-day national conference on Black boys and Black men in June 2007 in Brooklyn. During the course of this decade-long work I have found myself answering questions from Black males of all ages, classes, sexual orientations, and educational backgrounds, about what they should be reading, what they should be watching, what they should be doing to redefine Black manhood in a way that is rooted in love, nonviolence—including a respect for the humanity of women and girls—and a belief in a higher power.

This work and these questions forced me, over time, to make a commitment to my own healing and growth, to being completely transparent about my own life, and—to paraphrase Gandhi—to strive to be the change we want to see in the world. And over time I found myself giving out, first, a reading list, then a film and documentary list, then other critical handouts. And because I have been blessed to travel America extensively, I found myself able to recite the examples of progressive and proactive Black male leaders who have created real models of success and empowerment for Black males: people like David Miller and LaMarr Darnell Shields with the Urban Leadership Institute in Baltimore; Jason Warwin and Khary Lazarre-White with the Brotherhood/Sister Sol in New York City; Bryan Echols and MAGIC in Chicago; the Mentoring Center in the Bay Area of northern California; and the magnificent example that is Barack Obama—husband, father, leader, visionary, man.

But what lingers with me most are the memories of all the Black males, younger ones and older ones, straight ones and gay ones, of all religious faiths, or not, who have told me publicly or privately that they need help, that they have little or no life skills, that they do not know what it means to be a man. Some of these males are going to be okay, but others have committed suicide or remain addicted to alcohol or drugs; some have wound up in prison or dead from gunplay; some have been abusive to women and girls; and some continue to be violent toward other Black males. It's fair to say that many of us have been waiting for something like *The Black Male Handbook* our entire lives. A recovering gangbanger put it to me this way recently: "We need life skills. There is nothing that is teaching us how to live. Everything is about surviving, or dying."

And that is why I decided to produce *The Black Male Handbook: A Blueprint for Life*. This is by no means a flawless book, and I take full responsibility for its shortcomings. It is a labor of love and a gift to Black boys and Black men, from some of the most brilliant Black male minds in America today. With no apologies, *The Black Male Handbook* is intended to redirect the talk and rhetoric away from seeing ourselves solely as victims. Yes, racism is alive and well in America, and we will forever challenge and critique it, no question. But if Black males are going to be empowered, that empowerment has to be proactive—and holistic. That is precisely why I began ending my speeches with what I would come to call six points of empowerment or development: spiritually, politically, economically, culturally, and in the areas of physical health and mental wellness. That framework is manifested in the essays in this book, which can either be read sequentially, or as separate pieces depending on your particular needs and interests as a Black male. But I sincerely hope you read the book from cover to cover, because I believe you'll be transformed by these provocative essays, all of which include concrete, step-by-step instructions on how you can heal, grow, think, and become a different kind of Black male. And at the back of this book I've made it a point to include not only those reading and film lists I mentioned, but also helpful tips on what to do if stopped by the police, as well as practical grooming, etiquette, and job interview tips.

Editor's Note

So as we say at our monthly Black and Male in America (BAMIA) workshops in New York City, every kind of brother is a brother, every kind of brother is welcome, and this compilation is for the brothers who are willing to be here, right now. None of us who are writing in *The Black Male Handbook* are perfect. I have been, in my journey on this planet, practically every kind of brother: fatherless but now a mentor to many; homeless but now a home-owner; a college failure and outcast but now a possessor of an undergrad degree and an honorary doctorate; a violent, abusive, and ill-tempered man-child but now a man, because of years of therapy, who advises and consoles those who've been physically violated and abused; I have been arrested and ridiculed, but now I am a lover of life and someone who does not take a single day for granted. What I got from *The Autobiography of Malcolm X* many years ago (the single most important book any Black male could ever read) I have applied to my being: that if you truly want to be redeemed, if truly want to change, you can, you will.

And you, I, we, must understand, deep in our souls, in our hearts, in our minds, that if we destroy ourselves we destroy us all, if we destroy other Black males we destroy us all, if we destroy Black women and girls we destroy us all. There is no other way to say this. We must turn the tide in another direction, we must become about love and life, and not hate and death. So, it is my sincere hope that *The Black Male Handbook: A Blueprint for Life*, will be that first new brick in building a new life, for yourself, for your family and community, and for the generations of Black males to come.

Kevin Powell
Brooklyn, New York
2008

1

Creating A Spiritual Foundation

By Lasana Omar Hotep

I had a dream I could buy my way to heaven
When I awoke, I spent that on a necklace
—Kanye West
"Can't Tell Me Nothing"

Among the running jokes in the Black communities: the amusement and amazement we share watching a recording artist who makes music about violence, sex, and drugs receiving an award on television and saying, "I want to thank God." The contradiction seems glaringly obvious. How could a person who glamorizes greed, misogyny, and violence be religious or spiritual? We are all sitting there at home wondering, "How can the same person whose lifestyle and artistic expression emphasizes hatred, materialism, and raw intimidation, be standing there on-stage wearing a diamond-encrusted crucifix?"

Actually, this phenomenon provides an important insight into the complexity of Black male spirituality. The disconnection between what this individual practices and what he preaches (or believes) is not difficult to recognize. But recognizing a man who, regardless of his flaws, yearns to experience the unconditional love that only a higher power can supply may be more challenging. The source of this apparent contradiction can be traced to the way in which many of us are first introduced to religion and spirituality.

We are encouraged to worship from early in our development. But few of us are introduced to the concept of character development as an expression of spirituality. Some of us have become so focused on our particular religion that we lose sight of achieving *spirituality*. Religion is the set of rituals and practices used to recognize, worship, and seek communion with God. Spirituality is the manifestation of this divine connection in one's daily life. Think of religion as the vehicle and spirituality the destination. The destination is the ability to see aspects of God in our lives and to exhibit this awareness as we interact with our environment.

Although it may be easy for us to detect the contradiction in what a musician on an awards show does and says, it is often difficult to recognize it in our own lives. I first became aware of my personal contradictions at age fifteen. I was a fiery, up-and-coming Black Nationalist who thought he could change the conditions of Black life by overpowering people with Black facts. I remember recounting a ciphering (informal discussion) session that I had in the school cafeteria to one of my mentors. I was excited to explain to him how I had "blasted" all the brothers and sisters with my knowledge, and how stupid I made them look. He simply asked me, "What do we call each other?" I replied, "Brother and Sister." My mentor then asked me whether my actions seemed truly "brotherly." Without further discussion, I got the point. Just intellectualizing or articulating a concept wasn't enough. I also had to demonstrate it in my behavior. There it was staring me in the face: I was talking about being a "brother" but living out the life of a sarcastic smart-ass. It's not enough to talk the talk, you've got to walk the walk. From that point on I've used the same test as a measure for self-criticism and for my evaluation of society—especially religion.

I was not raised in a religious household. Growing up between Los Angeles and Long Beach, California, my family attended church primarily on two occasions: funerals and Easter. Unfortunately I attended my fair share of funerals. During the 1980s, Los Angeles was becoming the gangbanging and drug-slinging capital of the world. I had a father, uncle, aunt, and cousins involved in street life and they exposed me to some of the worst that the world has to offer.

Having these people in my life helped me to understand how young entertainers could embrace a lifestyle reflecting hatred while simultaneously professing a love for God. My family members were neither monsters nor soulless, uncaring people. They may have been into the streets neck deep, but they still wanted to be loved unconditionally. The love they received from family members was conditional and usually peppered with destructive criticism. But even in the midst of a destructive lifestyle, they turned to God for unconditional love.

But even as brothers seek this divine unconditional love, they who experience all the ugliness in the world still have issues with God. This is why so many Black males are absent from the church. Numerous articles, books, and community forums are held to address this matter. Truth is, some of these brothers are angry with God. Some are wondering where God was when they suffered abuse as little boys, or when they were mistreated as teenagers, or even now, when they are dismissed as shiftless adults—regardless of their personal struggles and/or successes. Others wonder where God was when they were being racially profiled by police, discriminated against in the workplace, or even when they found out their lover was cheating on them.

We know this anger exists because of the way Black men

murder one another without a second thought, the way Black males abuse girls and women, and the way we self-medicate with everything from alcohol to codeine-laced cough syrup, marijuana, and crack. The anger is manifest in our perpetual petty beefs, our judgmental attitudes toward other Black men, and our inability to constructively resolve conflicts among one another. The anger expresses itself in various other ways, too. Some Black men echo our oppressors and accuse fellow Black males of using racism as a crutch. Some may have enduring patience with other people who abuse and mistreat them, but have a short fuse when dealing with our Black brothers. These same attitudes can be found in men whether they were raised as Christian, Muslim, Hebrew, Buddhist, Humanist, African Spiritualist, or something in between. Indeed, this spiritual crisis is not merely a reflection of their character, but also of the religions and spiritual systems and institutions that claim to offer solutions to their problems.

In my own search for balance and centeredness I have rounded the bases of the world's most popular religions. At age fourteen, I left home plate and headed for Christianity as first base, joining a nondenominational storefront church congregation after attending services with an aunt. Like most young Black men, I wanted to have a strong relationship with God. During the devotional part of the service it was made clear that unless "you know, that you know, that you know" that if you died that instant you were saved and on the path to heaven, you risked burning in the fires of hell for eternity by not joining the church. I was not certain, so I joined. I went to new members classes and participated in youth activities. But, ultimately I found the experience to be unfulfilling.

I loved the fellowship and the message of hope the church preached and, yes, the music was incredible. I found an emotional release in the midst of community worship, but the generic sermonizing about God's power, grace, and vengeance missed me for the most part. As much as the pastor attempted to make biblical stories relevant to our daily lives, I still felt like he was talking about a time and place far removed from the reality I faced every day. Some brothers have issues with the church because of politics or other philosophical differences; I was too young to make those connections. I rather longed for something that spoke directly to my struggle as a young Black male trying to define my manhood, my Blackness, and my relationship with God in a constructive way.

At age fifteen, I left the Christian church for second base, the Nation of Islam (NOI). It was not an immediate transition. I spent several months in a kind of spiritual limbo. My experience as a Muslim awakened my spirit and my mind—not necessarily the theology of the Honorable Elijah Muhammad and Minister Louis Farrakhan—but with the social and political message of Black self-determination. By this time my mother had relocated us to San Antonio, Texas, in hopes of providing my younger brother and me with a safer environment. As already stated, inner-city Los Angeles in the late 1980s was a war zone and the casualties were predominantly young Black men.

I learned about the Nation via its weekly publication, *The Final Call*. Prior to reading excerpts of speeches by Minister Farrakhan, I had never heard a Black man mix politics, economics, sociology, and religion into such a digestible cocktail. I responded to the NOI because it was unapologetically Black. The Nation combats the identity issues that plague Black males by telling us that we are "the makers, the owners and cream of the planet earth," and moreover, that Allah (God) is Black and wants us to reclaim our legacy as rulers of the earth. The Fruit of Islam (FOI), the men of the NOI, are structured in a hierarchical quasi-military fashion that fulfills our yearning for belonging to a structured group. The selling of newspapers, bean pies, and other products places Black men in a constructive posture within the community. Not everyone likes bean pies, but whenever they see the young FOI approaching in a suit and bow tie, they nevertheless show respect.

Religiously, I practiced the prayers, attended the services and observed Ramadan (a Muslim time of fasting). The ministers who officiated the Sunday meetings used both the Bible and Qur'an. They made these texts speak to my circumstance by interweaving passages from scripture with Black history, interpretations of economic exploitation, and critiques of contemporary leadership for failing to empower the Black community. I remained an active, faithful Muslim into my freshman year of college.

A combination of forces moved me to the next base and separated me from the Nation of Islam. During the early 1990s, the NOI was going through some administrative and organizational restructuring. I was forced to choose sides: whether to stay with the minister who introduced me to the teachings of the Honorable Elijah Muhammad or to follow through with the changes being implemented by the national headquarters. After some soul-searching I realized that I was drawn to the NOI's Black empowerment ideology, but not necessarily the religion of Islam. I was becoming more of an independent thinker. I was also becoming interested in ideas, philosophies, and teachings that were not in the tradition of the NOI. And so I respectfully discontinued my active membership in the organization while I continued to hold steadily to the message of self-love and other empowering elements embedded in me by the NOI.

By the age of nineteen. I was off to third base. I had enrolled in Texas State University, and thus began a phase of experimentation and research. I reengaged with the church through the teachings of Black Christian Nationalism. I never joined the Shrine of the Black Madonna Pan-African Orthodox Church (PAOC), but I was intrigued by the concept of Jesus as a "Black Revolutionary Messiah." The PAOC was founded by Jaramogi Abebe Agyeman (formerly Albert Cleage, Jr.), a Black Nationalist preacher from Detroit and a close friend of Malcolm X. The PAOC provided valuable community services through their bookstores, museums, and youth programs. And its focus on self-determination, nation building, and embracing African culture made it very different from my previous church experiences.

Walking into the Houston shrine sanctuary was a truly transformative experience. The entire wall behind the pulpit is a mural of a Black Jesus with an Afro and carrying a walking stick. The PAOC teaches that Jesus was a Black revolutionary combating the social injustices of his time. Therefore, Black Christians are obliged to continue this great legacy of resistance to exploitation and injustice—using Jesus as the model revolutionary.

As riveting and empowering as the message of the PAOC was, I was beginning to realize that spirituality existed outside the Judeo-Christian and Islamic realms. In baseball terms, I was rounding third and heading home. My visits to the college library exposed me to the wealth of information available—not only about our African legacy, but also that of other cultures and worldviews. I started to read about Eastern spirituality, especially Zen Buddhism. From these spiritual systems I gathered a better understanding about the importance of taking time to meditate and clear my mind. That is literally what Zen means, to meditate. Meditation helps a person to still their mind and reminds us that our own desires are the source of our suffering. In Buddhism there is no God to be worshipped. The focus is not on paying homage to a creator but rather on each individual attaining enlightenment.

This concept was so empowering to me. It offers a spirituality based on how one behaves, not on what one professes. Demonstrating enlightenment is about walking the walk, not just talking the talk. The ultimate source of power is not external but inside each individual. All of us hold the power to either "do" or "not do." Exposure to these concepts and practices prepared me to be receptive to other life-changing spiritual experiences.

At age twenty-four, two years after graduating from college, I went on an educational tour of Egypt—or KMT, as the ancient inhabitants called it, meaning "The Black Land." I was motivated by the reading I'd done and lectures I'd attended espousing the fact that Egypt was an ancient African civilization built by Black people. But pictures and speeches did the real thing no justice. Standing in the presence of the Sphinx (Heru-em-akhet), the pyramids, and the temples was truly awe-inspiring. We have a saying in our community of "doing things big." Well, our ancestors did things "colossal." Everything was built to skyscraper scale, and the temples were covered in writings telling some of the earliest stories of spirituality and human consciousness. My Egyptian experience ignited a fire inside me to seek out the key principles of African spiritual systems.

I continued my personal spiritual investigation by exploring African spirituality, primarily the practice of Ifa. My appreciation for Ifa, the religion of the Yoruba people of Nigeria, came in phases. First I attended a ritual on the beach in Galveston, Texas, to pay homage to our ancestors who were brought to the shores of North America as slaves. The event was an interfaith affair with prayers and comments shared by clergy from various religions, but an Ifa priest performed the rituals. I had been in the Black Nationalist community for some time and was familiar with libations from ceremonies like Kwanzaa, but this was different.

The libation (prayer performed while pouring liquid) was

done in the Yoruba language accompanied by African drummers. Various other elements completed the ritual—corn symbolizing abundance, cowrie shells symbolizing prosperity, and yellow flowers symbolizing Yemoja, goddess of the sea. As "conscious" as I thought I was, I was very naïve to African spirituality. I had been taught, like many Black people in America, to dismiss our traditional religious systems as "voodoo" or "mumbo jumbo," vestiges of the evil jungles and the Dark Continent. Experiencing this powerful ceremony with its reverence for ancestors, prayers, dance, and song provided me with a fresh reorientation to traditional spiritual systems.

Later that year I received an invitation to attend the birthday celebration of an Ifa priest, which would include a "Ceremony of Ceremonies." At the Ceremony of Ceremonies I was able to see the diversity of traditional African spiritual systems. I met priest, priestess, and devotees (people vying for initiation) from a broad spectrum of systems practiced in the Caribbean, Latin America, and Africa. During the ceremony I witnessed a phenomenon that convinced me Black people are not as far removed from mother Africa as we might like to think. A Haitian priestess became possessed with the spirit of a deity and began to speak to us in *kreyol*. I immediately made the connection between this phenomenon and the Christian tradition of "catching of the Holy Ghost" and speaking in tongues.

These experiences intrigued and enlightened me, but not enough to become a devotee of Ifa and seek initiation. What fundamentally altered my perspective on African spiritual systems was the discovery of the Odu Ifa. The Odu Ifa is a collection of *odus* (Yoruba sayings) used by the *babalawo* (priest) to provide counsel. Some might call them scriptures. First and foremost the *odus* are profound in their own right. But perhaps more importantly they demolished the notion that we had no religion before the coming of Arabs or Europeans. The Odu Ifa affirmed my belief that Africans brought the world its first spiritual systems.

The Christian church taught me the power of collective worship, Islam taught me that spirituality can be empowering, Buddhism armed me with the tool of meditation, and African spirituality revealed the power of my ancestry. But the real home run for me was not practicing one particular religion, but rather embracing a broader concept of spirituality. That is what led me to home plate.

My spiritual journey thus far has led me from the church to the mosque to meditation to now a simple prayer table. The path taken has allowed me to see the universality and connectedness of religions and spiritual systems, and helped me understand why all people have a right to worship God in their own unique way. Respecting the universal truths that bind most religions gives me a low tolerance for religious chauvinism. And all the while I have found myself becoming more focused on the fact that the external expression of worship is not as valuable as one's internal commitment to living a life reflecting self-love, self-respect, and a commitment to service.

Some may interpret my spiritual journey as the wandering of a fickle, noncommittal, misguided young brother. Those who defend a particular religion (or "vehicle") may be reluctant to acknowledge that there are many roads leading to the ultimate destination of spirituality. But I would argue that my rich, diverse spiritual experiences have helped me understand why so many Black males distance themselves from organized religion. Some brothers are no longer convinced that their religion equips them with the tools they need to be successful in today's society.

The twenty-first century calls for a new manifestation of faith, one measured less by adherence to doctrine and more by living a life that is healthy and balanced in all aspects—physically, mentally, and spiritually—both in our families and in our community. We no longer live in a society governed by superstitions, age hierarchy, and unquestioned compliance with tradition. There are Black males who have become increasingly critical of religion as a whole, and they express their discontent in various ways depending on their personality. The less confrontational brothers simply abandon the church, mosque, or temple altogether. The more aggressive ones become cynics with a general disdain for religion. These are the brothers who consider anyone perpetuating religion to be a pimp or con man.

There are three fatal flaws found in most religious practice, which, if they were properly addressed, could alter Black men's perspective toward our spiritual systems.

One is our tendency to confine "holy" acts to our religious centers. We fill churches throughout the country—be they megachurches or small community congregations—adorned in our Sunday best. We gather in houses of Afro-Caribbean spiritual systems such as Voudon, Yoruba, and Candomblé, or attend rituals in rural areas in our beads and traditional attire. The Muslims among us attend Juma services. And Hebrew groups, both orthodox and Black Hebrew Israelites, gather in pockets throughout the Black community.

But once we leave that space, do we remember our values and principles? Many have come to believe that beyond the confines of the sanctuary, it isn't necessary to act out of one's higher self. Consider all the sensational cases of scandals in which religious leaders have been guilty of adultery, abuse, and financial mismanagement. Of course this "saint in the temple, sinner outside" syndrome applies to the congregation as well as the clergy. How many churchgoers relate to their families and communities in negative or destructive ways? The only justification for this schizophrenic behavior is the notion that spirituality can be confined within four walls rather than extending into our everyday lives and inter-actions.

This particular point was underscored for me when a friend of mine was choked by her husband while she was preparing to attend a religious service—in front of their children at that. One moment the family was getting dressed to go worship God, the next, mom was being strangled and dragged through the house by dad. On another occasion a priest made romantic advances toward another female friend under the guise of healing her. These situations and countless others remind us of the need to carry our spirituality beyond our places of worship.

As quiet as it is kept, there is an underlying politics of fear playing itself out in our religions, encouraging followers to be obedient so as to avoid punishment in the afterlife. Many of us think of our devotion as premiums that we pay into a sort of sacred insurance policy. We attend religious services, praise the higher power, and read our divinely inspired text. From this formula we hope to become beneficiaries of divine grace in life, while our spiritual benefactor awards prosperity in the afterlife. Ultimately, we are investing in security for when we die.

This fear-based argument is compelling. Death is the only experience guaranteed to all people regardless of race, gender, or socioeconomic status—and it is a mystery. Mortality stares us all in the face. This fear of the unknown played a major role in my submitting to the church as a teenager. The idea of "knowing that you know that you know" weighed heavily on my heart. But even when I was a Baptist I still felt as if there was more to learn. Although I was in the arms of salvation, I didn't feel any better prepared to survive in the world as a young Black man. So, yes, I thought my religion would save me from the fires of hell but I was uncertain that it could show me how to make it in the here and now.

Mortality was a real consideration in my family. My two maternal uncles both died at age twenty-two, one from a drug overdose and another from murder. My paternal grandfather and maternal grandmother recently died from lung cancer. Just three years earlier I remember crying until my eyes swelled when notified of the drowning death of my seven-year-old cousin. I had long come to terms with the fact that I could soon be the person on the cover of the funeral program. But the struggles not to fall into the traps of drugs and premature parenthood, while still making enough money to go to school looking clean, led me to gamble with my place in the afterlife.

Our willingness to test the boundaries of fear-based religions is quite apparent in rap music, an effective gauge of the Black male state of mind. In 2Pac's 1996 song "Hail Mary," Young Noble and Kastro of the Outlawz chant:

> *If it's on then it's on,*
> *We break beat-breaks*
> *Outlawz on a paper chase*

A similar sentiment of getting yours now and letting the chips fall where they may after death is also reflected in Nas's verse on the 2002 release "Life Is What You Make It," when he states:

> *No tears if I'm dumped in a hearse, I won't be the first*
> *Nor the last ni***, let's get this cash ni***.*

Rap is not the only music forum where Black men ponder our relationship with the divine. Through all of our musical forms—spirituals, jazz, reggae, rhythm and blues—we express our wrestling with mortality. Consider Al Green's transition from R&B crooner to gospel artist, or Sam Cooke's lyrics on "A Change is Gonna Come":

It's been too hard living but I'm afraid to die
'Cause I don't know what's up there beyond the sky . . .

Black men often feel hopeless. The realities of living in a society rooted in injustice, inequality, and racism—the secular—can take precedence over our fear of what's to come after death—the religious. Black men have been waiting for a change to come since we were brought to the Americas to work until death. We were denied full citizenship after the Civil War and the compromised fall of the Reconstruction era. The entire Black community had to endure the terror of lynching and rape during the hellish Jim Crow era. Both the nonviolent Dr. Martin Luther King, Jr., and the Black Nationalist Malcolm X died from gunfire. During the Black Power era our male leadership was incarcerated, exiled, and murdered. After inheriting this legacy of racism and injustice, how much worse can hell be?

Displaying good character as a means of avoiding retribution after life is not just problematic but inherently selfish. The idea of "personal" salvation is the third challenge facing contemporary religions. The old adage "I came into this world by myself and will leave by myself" is popular among those who seek to justify their self-centered lifestyle. But how a person enters or exits this plane of existence is not the issue. The fact is we live our lives among others. The issue is that many of the religions we practice stress individual salvation.

Presenting personal salvation as the aim of all spirituality is also reflective of a society focused on material acquisition. Those who move through the world looking out for number one tend to see other people either as barriers to individual progress or pawns to be manipulated. This belief system allows people with education, material wealth, and social status to neglect those who are unable to attain those privileges. It also provides comfort to those who live out an "American Gangster" fantasy by selling drugs to members of their own community. This type of attitude allows them to be indifferent to their fellow man as long as they keep their own personal salvation on layaway.

This indifference is a problem within the total society, resulting in violence and death among many young brothers in the inner city. Feelings of alienation, marginalization, and isolation cause some of us to adopt a "me against the world" mentality. That's why our spiritual systems and religions should reinforce the connections between us. Our commitment must not just be to ourselves but also to the condition of the collective. Let service to people be our way of serving God.

Whenever I have the opportunity to empower people through a workshop or lecture, I always try to change "I" to "we." I feel most connected to the Divine when I am developing and implementing success programs for African American males, both at the local and national level. When one of my students had a psychotic episode and I had to sit with him in a hospital room for thirteen hours to keep him from being forcefully restrained, I put aside the conveniences of the "I" for the well-being of the "we."

Many of us are familiar with the selfless spirituality of Dr. Martin Luther King, Jr., and Malcolm X. That same selflessness can be found in the lives and work of Dutty Boukman, one of the early leaders of the Haitian Revolution; the Honorable Elijah Muhammad, messenger of the Nation of Islam; and the civil rights activist Jaramogi Abebe Agyeman. From liberating slaves to building enduring institutions, these men demonstrated the power of seeking redemption for the collective as opposed to just the individual.

I could continue with a list of other challenges faced by our current religious institutions, but addressing these three areas would be a great start toward improving the lives of Black males:

- Stop thinking of divinity as limited to the confines of a building.
- Stop building our faith on fear of damnation.
- Stop seeking personal salvation above the good of the whole.

If we could do these things, our community might begin to reverse the trends that have made so many Black males distance themselves from religion. Our community is suffering and our success will depend on how we respond with solutions.

We now have a foundation upon which to build a transformational approach to spiritual thought and practice dedicated to producing the kind of Black males who can be assets to our communities and to the world. In an effort to reclaim our humanity, let us find new motivation for living by opening our minds to broader concepts of spirituality. No longer can the conservative clergy continue to argue that our people suffer because we aren't following the doctrines of old. If the old ways were enough, we would not face the grave challenges before us today. Our steps toward a more productive spiritual path begin with recognizing the need for change. We can no longer afford to seek analog solutions to digital problems.

I propose these five steps as starting points toward pursuing spiritual growth and wellness:

1. Set aside a place in the home to reflect, meditate, or pray.

2. Consume media (whether print, audio, or visual) content that promotes good character and balanced living.
3. Measure spirituality by cultivating harmonious relationships, not just by attending services or participating in rituals.
4. Practice forgiveness of yourself and others.
5. Perform acts of service within your family and your community.

These five steps aim to provide practical, meaningful ways to reconnect one with one's higher spiritual consciousness. I can offer no guarantee other than this one: There is no cure for everything. Any religious or spiritual system claiming to be the be-all-and-end-all is guaranteed to fail. It's not about abandoning your current religious practices, but about taking the first steps toward overall spiritual empowerment.

We can transfer the same relationship we have with our various religious centers (whether church, mosque, or temple) into our homes by designating a place in our home for reflection time, meditation, and prayer. This space should contain items you consider sacred, anything that speaks to your higher self. These might include spiritual texts, pictures or other symbols of your ancestors, and incense or candles.

Once you have created a sanctuary in your home, it can serve as a place to retreat during times of both frustration and elation. Choose a consistent time to sit at your prayer table or altar for at least fifteen minutes a day. You must give yourself enough time to become spiritually centered. On your most challenging days, one can vent in this space. During prosperous times, one can reflect on one's good fortune.

Whether you are climbing the corporate ladder, earning college credits, working part-time at the mall, or counting down days on an incarceration bid, a man needs a place where he can clear his head. This transfers spirituality out of a particular building and creates an immediate space for self-reflection rather than worship. In your religious center, in the company of your fellow believers, you offer external praise; at your prayer table or altar your attention is inward.

I sit at my prayer table every day, and I always find a way to use that time constructively. Some days I just sit and meditate to clear my mind. Other days I pray for family and friends who may be in need. Sometimes I reflect on the past or visualize my upcoming day. When I am stressed I simply breathe and think of a positive way to solve my conflict. Sometimes I read scripture or inspirational quotes. The important thing is to seize time out of your schedule to tap into your spirit.

Taking time for a self-inventory is a necessary first step toward making the transition from a religion focused on belief to a spirituality based on behavior. Our behavior is influenced by our environment. One of my mentors, Pastor K. Hakim Kokayi of Transformation International Church, has stated, "What you consume is what you will consider." According to this logic, if one wants to be whole, healthy, and productive, one should seek out and digest information that encourages such attributes.

Exploring spiritual texts, including traditional holy books— from the Bible to the Qur'an, the Torah, Odu Ifa, and Husia—can provide a basis for positive thinking. Readings can vary from scriptures, meditations, or literature, discussing the application of spiritual laws and principles. Both fiction and nonfiction materials offer insight on spiritual health and wellness. Writers like Ayi Kwei Armah, James Redfield, and Alice Walker include spiritual themes in their work. Howard Thurman, Deepak

Chopra, Iyanla Vanzant, Angel Kyodo Williams, and Kahlil Gibran sprinkle their writings with insights from diverse spiritual perspectives.

Listening to music that speaks to one's higher self also contributes to a more positive outlook on life. While spirituals and gospel music offer a traditionally religious message, other forms of spirituality can be found in the uplifting music of artists like Miriam Makeba; Bob Marley; Stevie Wonder; Earth, Wind & Fire; Femi Kuti; and India.Arie, to name but a few. Jazz music—also known as African American classical music—by the likes of John Coltrane and Thelonious Monk conveys powerful spiritual messages beyond words through instrumentation.

Some traditionalists may insist there is no redeeming value in "secular" music. But recent history has shown that a steady diet of gospel music does not exempt anyone from making destructive choices. From Kirk Franklin's pornography addiction to the domestic violence involving evangelists Juanita Bynum and Thomas W. Weeks III, it's clear that tuning out secular music is not a guarantee of righteous behavior.

Visual information plays as profound a role in shaping our environment as does sound. Seek to fill your home with images that reflect tranquility, preferably scenes from nature. I use images of beaches, rivers, lakes, mountain ranges, and tropical forests as computer screen savers to combat the cold concrete environment of the city. Our history is full of great women and men, ranging from Harriet Tubman to Malcolm X, whose images we can place in our homes, offices, and communal spaces. These ancestors serve to remind us of our rich cultural heritage and of the fact that so many people before us have done more with less.

Diversify your television and film consumption with documentaries, educational programs, and stories of spiritual growth. Turn off the reality shows and music videos and scan the History

Channel, Discovery Channel, or PBS for shows that broaden your understanding of the world and your role in it. For a candid interpretation of Black manhood and a serious look at our religious struggles, check out the St. Claire Bourne film, *John Henrik Clarke: A Great and Mighty Walk*. Give your spirit the break it deserves from the mediocre, dumbed-down entertainment that dominates popular culture.

Malcolm X remains the shining example of a Black man making the transformation from a menace to society to a minister to society. History tells us that Malcolm surrounded himself with books, articles, and anything he could find to feed his intellectual and spiritual curiosity, and to facilitate his metamorphosis. Within one lifetime he went from man-child Malcolm Little, to street hustler Detroit Red, to fiery Minister Malcolm X, to Omowale, an ambassador of Black Americans, to the mature lover of humanity, El Hajj Malik El Shabazz. Know that you too can obtain spiritual development within the context of your current situation (whether corporate, laborer, student, or artist) by being more selective about what information you place into your mind.

Rethink the way we measure our spiritual development. It is time we transform the notion of being saved by conversion, of taking oaths and submitting to rituals, and move beyond symbolic gestures into real-life practices.

Let's foster harmonious human relationships. What good is it to claim allegiance to a particular deity if you are unable to hold a peaceful conversation with your relative or spouse? Pay attention to relationships with the people in your life. Are they unstable, fragile, or volatile? How have you contributed to this problem? How can you counteract it?

Conflicts have an interesting way of telling us where we stand in terms of maturity and spiritual development. As conscious and aware as I considered myself to be, I had a tendency to raise my voice in conversations with my wife when I felt my point was not being understood. My wife felt my tone was disrespectful. She, on the other hand, never raised her voice during our conversations. I took her critique to heart, changed my behavior, and brought harmony into our relationship.

Reevaluate your man-to-man relationships. When we exhibit unhealthy competitive postures toward one another, it fosters petty jealousy and divisions. This egotistical attitude makes a simple thing like acknowledging someone else's accomplishments or successfully working together virtually impossible. Some of us could stand to have our perception of "manhood" realigned. If our notions of manhood include a desire to control every situation, or they leave us unable to let go of grudges, then we may be destined to have fractured relationships. Even if we cannot forget wrongdoing, real or perceived, we can let go and live and grow. There is hope in the practice of forgiveness.

Forgiveness means we don't allow disagreements to make us distrustful and guarded and the basis for all human interactions. When we don't forgive, we trap ourselves in spiritual prisons. On the other hand, forgiveness of one's self and of others opens up the doorway to new possibilities. Acts of forgiveness include apologizing or accepting apologies, offering amends, and simply releasing the hold that a particular situation has over your life. This is an especially effective spiritual approach for Black males who have issues with their father.

As a result of my father's substance abuse he suffered many losses, including his relationship with my mother. Their relationship was fractured but I always maintained contact and a relationship with him. He was a voracious reader who always sparked my curiosity to learn. He also has a contagious sense of humor so

I was able to bond with him beyond his addictions. My father has recently recovered from his addictions, and to this day he and I remain close and supportive of each other.

My father and I are lucky, but I still consistently run into Black males who were raised primarily by their mothers or grandmothers and who have serious problems with their fathers. Deeply scarred by the absence of their father, they hold on to the hurt, disappointment, and frustration. My words to them are: Brothers, you are not going to get those lost experiences back. Nor are you hurting him with your anger. Release yourself from the prison of hatred. *Forgive him.*

Beyond forgiving is giving. Performing acts of service to our brothers helps to reaffirm a bond lost through individualist beliefs and attitudes of distrust. Service can be given in various ways: tutor or mentor youth, help elders go to doctor appointments, host fundraisers for community projects, design programs for small business development, coach Little League, provide pro bono counsel, or allow someone to apprentice under your leadership. It all comes down to, "each one teach one."

When we share our own time for the benefit of the collective, we are centered in our higher selves. The unique spiritual satisfaction that volunteers derive from their work, far beyond any material compensation, is the beauty of giving back. Although our community has many allies, most of the work toward empowering Black males must come from Black males. And nowhere is our love of God more evident than through acts of service.

For the past four years, I have facilitated a monthly Black male study group that focuses on what it means to be Black and male in twenty-first-century America. Divine self-awareness is developed in these conversations, processing issues ranging from masculinity and sexuality to power and racism. The study group provides a context for these young brothers to engage the world both empowered and informed. Nobody pays to participate. These sessions are volunteer efforts, an act of service.

Money is not a prerequisite for opening. Dr. King stated that all one needs to serve is "a soul generated by love." While performing acts of service, we are no longer on the sidelines of life, saddled with fear and impaired by individuality. In reaching out beyond ourselves, we express a deep sense of communion with all that we honor as divine.

Many people argue that the Black man's salvation lies in economics, while others say politics. Still others advocate "knowledge of self." The truth is we need all of the above, and then some. Nevertheless, we trust in our spiritual foundation to sustain us through those times when finances, political power, and history cannot. I have witnessed relatives use their spirituality to divorce destructive lifestyles, recover from drug abuse, and pursue entrepreneurial endeavors. The key to their success was relying on the power within themselves rather than something external. In their bleakest hour, spirituality gave them a reason to live.

Our families and communities suffer because some of us do not understand the purpose of our lives. Society tells us to pursue wealth and power. Advertisements tell us the main purpose of life is to consume as much as possible. But if material possessions really brought happiness, why are so many wealthy celebrities unhappy and making decisions that lead them to incarceration and premature death?

To those who claim to be leaders and practitioners of spiritual systems, let your work be reflected neither in your material possessions nor by the number of individuals who follow your message. Let your success be measured by the character and humanity of your members and followers. Our stubborn loyalty to sacred buildings, fear-based pontifications, and self-centered salvation stare back at us in the eyes of our youth. Will we offer them hopelessness? Or will we be men of character, assets to our families and our communities? Will we demonstrate our unconditional love of God by how we treat those around us?

Regardless of the religious banner we prostrate ourselves beneath, men of African ancestry are facing a crisis individually and collectively. Of all the tools we have to repair our communities and ourselves, spirituality is the most powerful. Commitment to spiritual growth creates a firm foundation to build upon. We cannot afford to sit in judgment of brothers at the awards shows nor the brothers who sit in prisons because they emulated something they saw in a music video, or on the streets. Such are the spiritual challenges we face as Black males. This is a struggle that we must share collectively. Let us find meaning in our human existence through the reconstruction of Black manhood—physically, mentally, and spiritually. It's time to build.

2
Developing Political Awareness
By Jeff Johnson

I have spent the last decade developing and evolving my own political awareness. From my time as president of the Black Student Union as well as student government president at the University of Toledo, to serving as the national youth director of the NAACP, I have dedicated my life to empowering young people to create social and political change. I am humbled to be in the place I am today, where I can interview the likes of Barack Obama and the president of Sudan, Omar Al Bashir. But what is far more important to me is the humility I feel when meeting young men and women in our communities, whether they are directing programs and managing budgets or simply chillin' on the block. Young men and women who have been creating motivation in their local communities and even those suffering from the oppression of a society still driven by White racism. Many of these young men and women, regardless of circumstance, truly are "the BEST."

Being the BEST has little to do with a title you may have, how much money you have in the bank, or what you wear or drive. Being the BEST means that something we do is worthy to be shared with someone else. It means that the model that we are using can be taken and implemented for whatever institution, family, or program that needs it most. All too often we hear a lot of rhetoric about what should be done practically or theoretically, but we don't necessarily see a demonstration of actual work that has helped our communities, has changed lives, has affected retention rates, has raised graduation rates, has made young men on campus and in the community more successful not just as students, but as men.

Some of you are reading this like, "Come on Jeff, the people who are the best get paid, the people who are the best are on TV or famous, the people who are the best don't have to worry about the stuff that I worry about." Well, brothers (and those sisters who are reading), that is not the truth. How many of us can say that the best basketball player we have ever seen is locked up; or that the best singer we know is at the church? Don't let what society labels as the best confuse you. Hell, if we, especially as Black males, believed everything that we hear from the media and broader society regarding who we are and what is best for us, we would be in real trouble. So, as we deal with this whole "BEST" thing, what are we really talking about? Let's break it down:

B. The first thing we've got to deal with is B; we've got to blow up some things. When I go around the country, I hear too many Black men—even those in programs designed to empower Black males—who buy into stereotypes that aren't actually true. Programs that will attempt to destroy myths, yet will talk about the fact that there are more Black men in jail than in college. The reality is that there are more college-aged Black males in college than in jail. Too many of us deal with the fact that there are so many things wrong with African American men, but don't highlight the things that are right. We've got to blow up the stereotypes.

We've got to blow up some of our old standards, and not accept that because they are better than average, things are okay. The reality is there was a time when our grandparents and even our parents told us that we had to be twice as good when we showed up, because we had no choice. I went to a mixed high school in a suburb of Cleveland. The school was predominantly White, but was mostly tolerant of diversity. My parents were very clear with me that as a Black boy I had to be better, because in the eyes of too many, I was behind from the start. So it was not acceptable to bring home C grades when I had A potential.

But there are so many of us now that, when we go above what the average or the standard or the previous statistic is, we are comfortable with where we are, because it's better than where we've been. Until we blow up the mind-set that average and mediocre is acceptable, we will never manifest excellence.

We've also got to blow up the mind-set that we are competing against one another to do things that in many cases we need to be working together to do. We need to blow up the mind-set that we are the crabs in the barrel. When you keep talking about the crab in the barrel, you oftentimes become the crab. Stop talking about it and start putting brothers on your shoulders instead of focusing on the haters (crabs) that are *trying* to pull you down. I had a young brother ask me once at an event in Richmond, Virginia, "Why don't the crabs in that bucket use their claws to hold on to the top and pull each other out?" See, it is not about what you are, it's about how you see yourself and the responsibility you have to the people around you.

We've got to blow up the mind-set that allows us to use the

term "nigger" as a term of endearment. Even young men on college campuses act as if it's acceptable. I say "even" because institutions of higher education are places where we should be challenging traditional notions of what is acceptable and what is wrong. Young (and not so young) brothers, we cannot use that word in any way, shape, or form and disconnect it from the true definition and history associated with the word. I know we took the "er" off and put an "a" on the end. However our ancestors fought to provide us with the ability to use language so that we could speak life and not death into our situations. The term "nigger" should not be banned, but should never be confused with life. The slaves who were bought and sold, men and women who were legally lynched, and our grandparents who were blocked from opportunities that their U.S. citizenship promised—all this was made possible because they were considered niggers. If you believe that hiphop is so hot *and* fly that it has the ability to change history and justify the n-word as a term of endearment because you changed the spelling, you are an ignorant "nigger" who can't spell! We've got to get to the place where we understand that how we define ourselves from the beginning will determine where we are able to go in the end.

E. After we blow up that negative mindset, we've got to educate ourselves to engineer and erect institutions. There is a scholarship in the state of Georgia called the Hope Scholarship. The state uses lottery money to guarantee college for students with a B average who otherwise would be unable to afford it. That's *great!* There are other federal, state, and local government programs that look to help a few from our community who usually would have made it anyway. However, the state should not be our meal ticket to self-sufficiency. Until we as Black males begin to build institutions that fund and take care of themselves, we will constantly be waiting on funding to run out. And by the time that much of this funding runs out there may or may not be a provost or executor, governor or other "leader" who supports the kind of vision that we need in the Black community. Black people spend too much money in America not to have our own institutions and to continue to beg the federal and state government and local folks for funds. Not that we don't deserve them, but we should be using our own wealth to build our own institutions. We need to begin to engineer programs that go beyond superficial, cotton-candy programs to make people feel good but create no fundamental change. We've become so comfortable with the rhetoric of leadership that we never look for the very transformation that defines real leadership. We've got to begin to educate young men to change their thinking and the perception of what Black men are in the media to what we know Black men are supposed to be.

S. We've got to begin to create sophisticated strategies. Don't tell me that because something feels like the 1960s it's gonna work in 2008. What worked in the '60s worked in the '60s because people in the '60s understood that they had to create sophisticated strategies for . . . the '60s. But what does it mean when we have leadership that looks to excite us to a state of euphoric inactivity by bringing up strategies of the past that cannot work today? I want you, my brothers, to understand that there has never been a time when grandparents led a movement. Yes, grandparents have served as mentors. Yes, there have been elders who served as advisors. But they weren't soldiers on the front line. Anytime Big Mama is leading your movement, your movement ain't going to win. You've got to begin to use your intellect, your passion, your drive, and your ambitions—to create sophisticated strategies that change things that we know don't work. If it doesn't work, challenge it, and stop doing it. Adapt and overcome.

I've seen too many programs for young Black men where there were no young Black men involved developing the strategy. I don't know about you, but nobody knows how to fix my problems better than I do. So if we're talking about African American male initiatives, but there are no Black males making key decisions, then what kind of Black men do we invite? I'm tired of showing up at programs where all the males look a certain way. Where your hair must be a certain way, your clothes must be a certain way, and you must talk a certain way—or you are not welcomed in the program. I'd rather have a straight-up gangster kid off the block who's got the heart to create change, than a kid in a suit and tie who knows how to play the role, but isn't prepared to do any work. I'm less concerned about how young brothers dress and more concerned with them being covered with character.

How many of us know somebody who has made a mistake but rose from that low point to become a champion? How many of us know somebody who went to jail, but was able to come out and turn his or her life around? How many of us know a young person who flunked out of school, but had the gumption to come back and graduate? How many of us *are* that somebody who made more mistakes than we can count, but learned from those mistakes and came back? I was that brother. Even as an "adult" I have not always treated the women in my life the right way, or been the father that I should be. But every day I look beyond my mistakes to attempt to become better. That process never ends and I would encourage you to keep pushing even when no one else is watching. I see us ignoring too many young men who have made mistakes and learned from them, men who have the leadership abilities to help bring along more brothers who need to be in these programs. There is a place for every one of you in this movement.

Developing new strategy puts us in a position to create new results. As much as I value the contributions that both Jesse Jackson and Al Sharpton have made in their decades of service, we did not need another Black man like them running for president of the United States. What does that mean? Yes they should be dedicated, focused, and concerned about the well-being of Black people. However, they should not be the same type of activist carrying what is primarily a "Black agenda." We need those kind of leaders, but we needed to see a Barack Obama. In listening to and interviewing him, I realized that he was not a "Black leader," but rather a leader who happened to be Black. This change in strategy has allowed America (especially so-called "liberals" and "progressives") to test their own notions of equality in the real world for the first time. For Obama's candidacy is really about America. While he has taken opportunities to address the race issue, he has never worn it on his sleeve. I guess he figured it was already all over his face. Obama is now doing something many of us will have to learn: how to serve a larger calling while simultaneously fighting for our people. That is the sort of strategy we need.

T. We need to use our sophisticated strategies because then we will be able to get to the T and turn tragedy into triumph. I don't know about you, but I go all around communities in this country, whether it's Baltimore, whether it's Cleveland, whether it's Pittsburgh, whether it's Houston, whether it's Oakland, whether it's Atlanta, whether it's smaller towns and cities. So often I see the same thing: young men who are involved in violence, not because violence is fun, but because they don't feel like they have any other options. You can't cure violence with a candlelight vigil and a prayer service. You've got to cure violence with opportunity. You've got to change how young Black males look at themselves, and what their future has the potential to be.

If we are not dedicated to being the best, and changing tragedy into triumph, then what are we doing? Are we the kind of activists who are just interested in turning in an annual report at the end of the year showing that we properly spend the budget we were given—even if we didn't actually change anybody? Are you prepared to blow up what you thought was the traditional way of doing things? To erect new institutions and ways of thinking? To develop sophisticated strategies that can turn the tragedy of hopelessness into the triumph of hope? That will turn the tragedy of believing that *I'm a pimp, I'm a hustler, I'm a thug, I'm a baby-making machine, I'm a nigger,* into understanding that I could be a doctor, a lawyer, a mathematician, a scientist, a creator, *and* a father.

THE BLUEPRINT

So what should we be doing once we have embraced being the BEST?

Here are the six things I recommend:

1. *Eat right.* What we consume ultimately determines how strong our bodies and minds are. Similarly, the information and media content we consume determines how we view ourselves, and whether we are equipped to fight the social, political, and even personal battles that lie ahead. From books (and other reading material) to websites,

from movies to music—if you consume garbage, you exude garbage. The question is: Do you stink?

I remember when I first started the process of becoming more politically powerful. I had always been kind of a news nerd. I wanted to know more about what was going on in sports, politics—really everything—than my peers. Ever since middle school I watched the news religiously, but I was not exposed to anything that challenged me socially or culturally. I was born in Europe and had the benefit of being able to travel quite a bit. Even so, before the Internet, I was still consuming the same media (TV, radio, and movies) as the average American teenager. It was not until college that I became truly "enlightened." Not long after I was elected Black Student Union president at the University of Toledo, I changed my information diet. I started reading the Cointelpro Papers, declassified FBI papers that outlined their attack on most of the movement for Black power and equality in America. As I learned about Huey Newton, I wanted to read what he read, so I opened David Walker's *Appeal*, and then Frantz Fanon. I then learned of a man named Cheikh Anta Diop, who absolutely blew my mind with his exploration of the role diasporic people had played in world history. All that is to say . . . as my diet changed, so did my social and political strength. More importantly, I started looking at who I was and my personal importance to my community and family differently.

I can tell you countless stories of brothers and sisters who have experienced the same sort of growth as a result of changing their intellectual diets. But let me start by giving you a diet you can follow:

Newspapers: Read (or at least look at) three different newspapers a day (if that's too many to start with, try three a week).

Websites: BBC.com, AllAfrica.com, AllHipHop.com, and TheRoot.com.

Music: Listen to everything you can get your hands on and actually *listen* to it. Challenge yourself to question what you hear and what it means to you. Listen to music from eras and genres that you are not familiar with. The diversity will make you more diverse.

Magazines: *Worth* magazine (it's what the truly wealthy read). Get your hands on academic journals. Manning Marable has a great one called *Souls*, but there are several out there.

Books: You can never get enough, but here are a few I think you have to get your hands on:

> *In the Matter of Color: Race and the American Legal Process 1: The Colonial Period*, by A. Leon Higginbotham. In the words of the *Harvard Law Review*, the book "chronicles in unrelenting detail the role of the law in the enslavement and subjugation of Black Americans during the colonial period. No attempt to summarize the colonial experience could convey the rich and comprehensive detail which is the major strength of Judge Higginbotham's work."

> *They Came Before Columbus*, by Ivan Van Sertima. This book makes it possible for us to see clearly the unmistakable face and handprint of Black Africans in pre-Columbian America, and their overwhelming impact on the civilization they found here.

> *African Origin of Civilization: Myth or Reality*, by Cheikh Anta Diop. A classic that everyone reading this essay should study.

Developing Political Awareness

From Slavery to Freedom: A History of African Americans, by John Hope Franklin. A comprehensive and reader-friendly text.

The Alchemist: A Fable About Following Your Dream, by Paulo Coelho. A simple story that provides guidance to those who are attempting to follow the purpose for their life.

The Art of War, by Sun Tzu. Publisher Oxford University Press says, "Written in China over two thousand years ago, Sun Tzu's *The Art of War* provides the first known attempt to formulate a rational basis for the planning and conduct of military operations. These wise, aphoristic essays contain principles acted upon by such twentieth-century Chinese generals as Mao Tse Tung."

2. *Find your issue.* Spend a moment identifying the issue or issues (not more than three to start) that really moves you. What makes you mad, sad, frustrated, and the like? It is on the other side of that emotion that you will find the issues that are connected to your personal social/political action call. Don't be afraid if you're not sure where to start yet. It is easier to find something that moves you and then figure out how to be involved than to be in an organization or movement simply because it's there, but you don't believe in the mission. I started out as a pissed-off college student at the University of Toledo, one who felt like there needed to be services provided for Black students that were not provided. I got together with some amazing students, faculty, staff, and even community

members to create a series of changes that can still be seen at the university. We didn't know how we would start; we just knew that we cared. The Africana Studies department we worked to get on the campus has already celebrated ten years there. We found our issue . . . what's yours?

3. *Identify your agenda and capacity.* Once you know the what, then you can deal with the how. It is important that we assess our capacity before we develop our agenda. What CAN you honestly give today? Is it time or money? Is it your voice or your mind? Can you serve in an elected position, will you make it your profession, or simply be the most important ingredient—the volunteer? Decide what you can do today and then create a plan to do it. As you evolve so will your capacity.

4. *Connect with an institution or organization.* Many of us want to get involved but don't know where to start. I suggest finding a local organization that is consistent with the issue you care about, and has opportunities for you to give according to your capacity. But don't get it twisted. You don't *have* to roll with an organization. Just make sure your service is institutionalized. Meaning, is it sustainable? Will it go on even after you shift to something else or, God forbid, stop? Churches, community centers, schools, and local programs are all looking for good people. Just make sure they are doing what they publicize they do. If you're gonna be down, be down with people doing it the right way.

5. *Build a coalition.* As Black males we have often been told we can do things alone. Brother, we need one another. This includes our elders *and* our women. You cannot create change if women are on the sidelines. I am so tired of

going to panels and rallies that have zero to too few female voices and perspectives when our sisters make up such a large part of our community. We need sisters who are capable and willing to lead as much as we need brothers. But more important than that is that we have to respect one another in leadership. I have seen more sexist brothers in the movement (in leadership) than outside. Respecting our sisters has to translate into our personal lives if we want it to manifest in our social action.

We must also build relationship with "elders" even as we move "old folks" out of the way. Old people are simply those who feel like leadership is determined by how long you have been there, while elders understand that their time here is about touching the younger generation, so that the younger generation won't repeat the mistakes of the past. Elders have so much to contribute, but often we act like we know it all. I can't tell you how many mistakes I made as a young leader because I was unwilling in some cases to listen, and in other cases there was no elder there. Seek them out, brothers. Even the Bible says, "He called the young because they're strong, but the old because they know the way." Only together will we have strength guided by wisdom.

6. *Move.* Make no excuses. Just make change. If we are not willing to be the best, then we might as well just go home, because we're wasting our time. It's not just about proving to a funder that you've got a great program. It's also about the fact that Black males are dying. But some of us are prepared to do what it takes to change this country, as well as our communities and our streets and our homes, to be the best. Because what America is looking for is leadership. You see it in every young person who wants

P. Diddy to lead them to the polls and Jay-Z to lead them to the bank. You know that a nation is suffering from a leadership void when you are looking for artists and entertainers to lead you.

You all are the leaders of the community that we need. So what are you waiting for? *Lead.*

3

Redefining Black Manhood

By Byron Hurt

"**Close your eyes**," my father would tell my sister and me as we drove down the interstate through South Carolina toward our final destination of Milledgeville, Georgia, the state's capital prior to the Civil War. It was a yearly ritual, each time we drove down south. My father would turn down the Teddy Pendergrass on the eight-track player. "Imagine Black people working in these fields from sunup till sundown," he'd say, "bodies glistening with sweat." I'd shut my eyelids tight and imagine what my eyes had never seen in real life—*slavery*.

"Imagine Black men on each side of these roads, lifting huge bales of cotton, and Black women hunched over, working in the fields," he'd say. I'd sneak a peek and look to my right, then quickly to my left at the cotton fields just off the highway. Then he'd cap off the exercise with a personal challenge: "Now imagine it was *you* working in those fields!" It wasn't easy for an eight-year-old mind to grasp slave labor, but my vivid imagination could clearly see the picture my father painted for us. I daydreamed about my young body lifting big bags stuffed with cotton, overcome by the heat. I just couldn't understand why Black people had to work under such horrible conditions. For miles I'd sit in the backseat next to my sister, wondering what it must have been like to be a Black man back then. Soon, dad's music would get loud again, and I'd open my eyes.

My father and mother were both born in the South. They both lived through Jim Crow, a legal system of apartheid that kept my parents' Black world largely separate from the world of Whites. Whenever we drove "home," to Georgia, my dad wanted his children to understand the land they were traveling in and its history, including the legacy of slavery. He would tell us how Black people were sold from plantation to plantation, never to see their loved ones again, and how White men tied knotted ropes around the necks of Black men, and hung them from trees—for little or no offense.

As he talked about slavery, I could see my father's expressive eyes dim and hear the disgust in his voice, as he broke down a piece of history. He was a strong, dignified man, committed to his family, full of knowledge of Black culture, and he had a heart as wide as the ocean. He hated racial stereotypes of Black people and relished undermining them. He worked especially hard at demolishing the mean-spirited stereotypes of Black men that White people had historically conjured up. To counter them he always spoke eloquently, worked hard, stayed out of prison, owned his own home, and provided for his children. The son of a hardworking but neglectful and alcoholic brick mason, my father worked with his hands as a contractor and modeled hard work to my sister and me. But from a father to a son, he wanted to make sure he prepared me for what lay ahead.

"You gotta work twice as hard as the White man, Byron," he'd tell me, "especially as a Black male, if you want to succeed in this world." He emphasized education above all else, and he encouraged me to read and to learn about Black culture. On Sunday mornings, he'd have my sister and me walk to the corner store and pick up the newspaper and a *Jet* magazine. Stacks of *Ebony* and the NAACP's *Crisis* magazine lay scattered throughout the house. He wanted us to see positive images of Black people, particularly of Black men. Every Sunday afternoon we'd watch *Like It Is* with Gil Noble, a Black-produced news program that covered politics, current events, and cultural affairs. My father was a serious, focused man, and race and politics were his favorite subjects. Hanging around him, I knew that being Black and male meant something different than being White and male in America. His politics became my politics, and his sensibilities around race issues rubbed off on me. Like my father, I grew to become a race-conscious man obsessed with images of Black masculinity.

Like most Black males, I feel pain and anger when I see the daily assault on our collective image. I feel the hatred and hostility thrown toward Black men and Black boys every single day when I read the newspaper, watch television news, TV commercials, Hollywood movies, and television sitcoms. Some of it is subtle. Some of it is blatant. Conservative Whites (and conservatives of color) who are in denial about racism—or simply don't want to confront the reality of racism—would like Black men to believe that we are crazy, that these images are figments of our imagination. But don't let 'em play you, brother! You're not crazy. You're perfectly sane, and so am I.

The crazy ones are the White people—the Bill O'Reilly and Ann Coulter types—who tell us that racist images of Black males no longer exist. They claim that we are holding on to racism or "playing the race card" whenever we suggest that race is a factor in how White people frame and tell our stories in the mainstream media. But let me set the record straight here: amoral White people in positions of power in newsrooms, at television stations, and in Hollywood manipulate our image and play the "race card" every single day. Although some Black people are beginning to share power and influence with Whites in the media industry, Black people do not typically control the huge international media conglomerates that bombard the culture with images of Black males that are churned out daily for a global mass audience. White people with money, power, and influence do. White media perpetuates images of Black men that reinforce long-held stereotypes and beliefs about us.

Far from overreacting to these racist images, we Black males don't stand up often enough to challenge the negative portrayal of Black men in sports culture, hiphop culture, advertisements, entertainment, and other places where Black men can be seen in abundance. These carefully constructed images of Black men and Black boys make an indelible impact on how the people of the world view us, and most importantly, how we view ourselves as Black males.

I don't know about you, but I think about my Black maleness *everywhere* I go: walking down the street, in elevators, in stores, at the gym, in crowds, on trains, on airplanes, around other Black men, and especially around large crowds of White people. Even as a thirty-eight-year-old man, I can't seem to shake the fact that people from all racial backgrounds prejudge me before they even get to know me. Why am I so hyperaware of my Black maleness and the way other people perceive me? Because I know that so many people in this country have bought into the various stereotypical images of Black men as big, dangerous, and scary. From

Nat Turner to Jack Johnson, Marcus Garvey to Malcolm X, Jim Brown to Mike Tyson, O. J. Simpson to Bigger Thomas, Barry Bonds to Pacman Jones—we conjure up fear in the hearts of people who have not closely examined their prejudices of Black males. Meanwhile the media, from Hollywood movies to cable news, continue to play on White people's overwhelming fear of Black men.

Images of Black males in the media have been distorted for so long in this country that many of us don't even recognize dangerous images when we see them. We are desensitized to them because we see them so much in popular culture, and because they've become a part of the language of media. Indeed, many of us have been brainwashed to such a degree that we buy into these images and even perpetuate them, without even knowing it.

Actor Lincoln Theodore Monroe Andrew Perry, better known as Stepin Fetchit, played the role of a lovable but servile, shiftless, lazy, simple-minded Black man in the 1920s and 1930s, but in real life he was a hardworking, intelligent actor and writer. *The Birth of a Nation* is hailed by critics as a cinematic breakthrough and a great American movie, but D. W. Griffiths's blockbuster, made in 1915, spread fear and paranoia about Black men as lazy, untrustworthy, oversexed, and dangerous, particularly to White women—thus giving rise to a reenergized Ku Klux Klan. Many cultural critics have noted that the 1933 movie *King Kong*, a story about a giant Black ape falling in love with an innocent White woman, tapped into White people's unspoken fear of Black men's potent sexuality. That racially charged King Kong image persists and resonates even today. The controversial April 2008 *Vogue* magazine cover, shot by award-winning photographer Annie Leibovitz, features NBA superstar LeBron James and supermodel Gisele Bundchen in a pose reminiscent of the *King Kong* movie poster. Many critics have speculated that the James/Bundchen cover of *Vogue* was intended to conjure up this image of "the dangerous Black man."

So how did the images of Black males get this way, and what do we do to change them? Ever since the days of slavery, White people, especially White men in positions of power and authority, have had to figure out ways to control Black men in order to maintain power over us. Slave masters realized that they had to dehumanize Black men in order to justify enslaving Black men, beating Black men, selling Black men like cattle, and killing Black men, to warn other Black men that the same would happen to them if they did not "stay in line." These oppressive tactics enabled White men to maintain their authority and power over Black men. White men in positions of power and authority had to prove to everybody—White people and Black people alike—that Black males were inherently inferior. One tried-and-true way to "prove" that Black men were less than human was to create images that made Black males look bad and made White males look good. They created pernicious stories and told the world falsehoods through books and visual images that Black men were stupid, lazy, shiftless, and immoral beasts with no ability to control our sexual desires or urges.

Throughout the history of radio, film, and television, media makers, both White and Black, created images of us that inaccurately depicted who we were as a race and as a gender, making us look silly to the rest of the world. Over time, and through repetition, White people with the power to control our image made us believe that we were brutes, savages, bucks, buffoons, jesters, coons, and Uncle Toms. (Please read Donald Bogle's *Toms, Coons, Mulattoes, Mammies, and Bucks: An Interpretive History of Blacks in American Films* for a blow-by-blow account.) They told us that we were intellectually inferior, that our brains were smaller than the brains of White men. They told us that we were physical specimens capable of doing a lot of menial labor, but could not make good decisions. They said that we could not do the important things White men did, things like voting, owning land, or creating our own businesses. They essentially murdered any positive notions that Black people were fully human, like White people.

Of course Black people resisted these racist images of Black men in media. Oscar Micheaux, often regarded as the first Black filmmaker, made forty-four movies from 1919 to 1948 with the specific aim of counteracting negative Black male stereotypes. His film *Within Our Gates* attacked D. W. Griffiths's racist depictions. Historian Carter G. Woodson, known as the "father of Black history," established "Negro History Week" in 1926 to increase racial pride and challenge stereotypes of Black people. From the late 1800s into early 1900s, Black men from Frederick Douglass to Marcus Garvey published Black newspapers like *The North Star, The Chicago Defender, The California Eagle, The Afro-American, The Pittsburgh Courier,* and *The Negro World.* These newspapers covered news in the Black community, and told stories from a Black perspective. (Please watch Stanley Nelson's award-winning documentary film, *Soldiers Without Swords: The Black Press,* to learn more about Black newspapers.)

But despite the resistance of Black filmmakers and publishers, the negative images of Black males created by White media makers were powerful and pervasive enough to stick in the minds of people like glue. Over time, people of all racial backgrounds came to associate Black men with negative characteristics and negative behavior. Black males were viewed with suspicion, and perceived as untrustworthy, violent criminals. This perception of Black men has had a lasting effect, and pervades the minds of millions of people around the world even to this day.

Black males still have to prove to the world that we are not as bad as we're supposed to be. All these negative images were created for us, not by us. We can only fight against these racial stereotypes by countering negative images with positive ones. Still, the negative stereotypes of Black men persist, and it will take a great effort to challenge them. We can start by teaching Black males not to buy into them, to recognize when we see racist and demeaning images of us in the media. Black students must be taught media literacy (the art of "reading" media) to create awareness and critically deconstruct and decode the images we encounter on a daily basis.

As a young man, I was aware that Black males were viewed negatively in society. But it wasn't until I went to college in 1988 that I began to understand just how systematically people were being programmed to accept these negative stereotypes of Black men. During my senior year at Northeastern University, I took a course called "Blacks in the Media and the Press," which focused on images of Black people in cartoons, television shows, and in Hollywood movies. That class changed my life.

We watched the works of documentary filmmaker Marlon Riggs, whose films *Color Adjustment* (1989) and *Ethnic Notions* (1987) really blew my mind. Those films highlighted the ways in which Black people, including Black males, were stereotyped in the mainstream media, and the powerful impact these images had on society. Little did I know that some of my favorite cartoons, like *Tom and Jerry*, were loaded with racist imagery, from the female mammy character, Mammy Two Shoes (who famously shouted *"Taaaaaaaammmaaaay!"*), to the dark-skinned Black men with big red lips eating watermelon and spitting out seeds like a machine gun. I learned that some of the beloved 1970s TV sitcoms that I grew up watching, like *Good Times* and *That's My Momma*, reinforced stereotypes of Black men and women that dated all the way back to the minstrel era. Jimmy Walker's "J. J. Evans" character was a repackaged coon image, and Theresa Merritt's "Mama Eloise" character was a recycled mammy image. The class transformed my thinking. I never again looked at images of Black people in the media the same way.

Other African American Studies classes that I took throughout my college years made me much more conscious about race issues. No longer could I accept or tolerate racist thinking about Black people. I became very sensitive about the way people viewed me as a Black man, and I spoke up whenever I heard my White professors or White classmates say something that I perceived to be racist. I think some people thought that I was militant or too outspoken. But after reading books like *The Autobiography of Malcolm X* by Alex Haley, or *Jubilee* by Margaret Walker, how could I keep quiet? I learned about organizations born during the civil rights movement of the 1950s and 1960s—from the Student Nonviolent Coordinating Committee (SNCC) and the Southern Christian Leadership Conference (SCLC) to the Black Panther Party—and how young Black people organized to struggle against racism. I also learned about the Black Arts movement of the 1960s and early 1970s, which set out to redefine our place in the arts and popular culture. Spearheaded by poet and activist Amiri Baraka, the Black Arts movement was the artistic extension of the Black Power movement. A collection of Black writers and poets like Baraka, Larry Neal, Ed Bullins, Nikki Giovanni, Askia Toure, Maya Angelou, Sonia Sanchez, and others expressed Black rage at White supremacy, and they sought to reshape existing images of Black people in the media and the arts. The civil rights and Black Power movements found expression in the music of Black songwriters and recording artists like Nina Simone, Aretha Franklin, Sam

Cooke, Marvin Gaye, Curtis Mayfield, John Coltrane, Max Roach, the Last Poets, and many other giants.

As I learned about these movements, I began to understand who I really was as a Black man, and how rich and important my culture was. I became extraordinarily proud of my heritage. The more I learned about African people, African culture, and the greatness of Africans before we were captured, enslaved, and shipped to the Americas during the transatlantic slave trade, the more vocal I became about all the issues that affect Black males.

Although I respected Black women, I never really made a distinction between Black men's issues and Black women's issues. To me, the issues were all the same, but in reality, because I benefited from male privilege, I did not understand that there were differences in the ways oppression affected Black women. For me, race issues were synonymous with Black men's issues. Although I probably would not acknowledge this when I was a college student, I prioritized Black men's issues over Black women's issues. I felt that Black men were so under attack that Black people collectively had to liberate Black men from the oppressive grip of White men. Little did I know how sexist my thinking was at the time. Although my college girlfriend often called me out about my sexism, I resisted her. I didn't do much of anything to actively challenge my own attitudes and behavior, or those of my male friends, teammates, and fraternity brothers. Yet today I consider myself an activist, which means that I am a person who will speak out against both racism and sexism, including male violence against women.

People often ask me, "How did you go from being a quarterback to becoming an antisexist activist?" Well, here's how it all went down: I started playing organized football in the Police Athletic League (PAL) at age seven. Like most seven-year-old boys, I had no clue how to play the game. I knew nothing about basic technique, play calling, or form tackling. Hell, I didn't even know how to put my uniform on properly. The day our coach issued the team our pads, I put my thigh pads where my kneepads should have gone, put my kneepads where my thigh pads should have gone, and put my hip pads upside down inside my girdle. My coaches thought this was funny, but I shrugged it off. I was there to have fun. On the playing field, I avoided physical contact like I avoided taking cod liver oil. On offense, I ran the ball like a young Gayle Sayers—cutting on a dime with gazelle-like speed and quickness—just so no one would tackle me. On defense, I jumped on top of the pile at the end of each play—like Deion Sanders used to do—so I wouldn't have to tackle anyone. By traditional masculine football standards, I was very much the seven-year-old wimp.

I only joined the football team in the first place because Ernie Simpson—the oldest guy on my block—signed up to play. News of Ernie becoming a football player spread like wildfire. My friend Chris Babb and I were so impressed we begged and pleaded our parents to let us join, too. Ernie wasn't just any kid on the block. He was by far the toughest, most intimidating force in the *neighborhood*. Our respect for Ernie was deep, and was based mostly on our fear of him. He was older, cooler, and bolder than the rest of us. Plus, he was proficient at kicking our asses! Ernie was so menacing, he'd punk you right out of your shoes. Consequently, we made Ernie our leader. We all wanted to be him or at least a little like him, so Ernie's approval of us became essential. When Ernie joined PAL football, it influenced at least a dozen young Black boys to do the same, leading perhaps to the most dramatic surge of sign-ups in PAL history! Within one short week, it seemed like every boy in my town was a Central Islip Blue Devil.

Ironically, I was taught to throw a football by three girls: my twin babysitters Paulette and Bernette, and my sister, Taundra. The three of them took me out into the street, hurled the football toward me, and told me to catch it. Once the ball was in my arms, they shouted at me to throw it back. That's how I learned to catch and throw a football. So at football practice, when my adult male coaches yelled, "You throw like a girl!" I became confused. I thought Paulette, Bernette, and Taundra threw the ball just fine. But a football field was no place to question your coach, let alone raise issues about gender. And at seven years old, I didn't have the vocabulary, or the courage, to challenge my coach's gender bias. We did what we were taught to do. And I learned, very quickly, that older men didn't like us throwing, hitting, running, or standing around "like girls." In fact, we made sure to abolish any obvious "girlish" tendencies just to remove any doubt that we were real boys. Our greatest objective was proving our ruggedness and gaining our coaches' approval.

My coaches were not my only teachers when it came to learning about manhood. I had many, both on and off the football field. My older cousins, for example, personified two typically masculine attributes—strength and physical power. Like Ernie, Alan and Phillip had attained what most young males wanted: toughness. Achieving tough-guy status did not come easily if you were a Hurt. You had to earn it. This meant that us boys had to put in work. At family gatherings, Alan and Philip would pit my cousin Q against me, forcing us to wrestle. They would try to predict the winner, saying things like "I think Q can take Byron," or "I think Byron is stronger than Q." As the instigated wrestling ensued, if either of us showed signs of giving up or losing, they would yell at us repeatedly: "Don't be no *punk!*" When it was over, Alan and Phillip would chastise the loser for being "too soft," while the winner won their manly approval and respect. Win, lose, or draw—Q and I loved them both, and looked up to them.

Non-family members also made their impact on me. At home one night, the son of a family friend called me a "sissy" as I prepared to go to sleep in the same bed as Taundra. At that time, I didn't know what the word meant, but he said it with such negative energy that I knew it could not be anything good. His venomous words, followed by mocking laughter, cut through me like a razor blade. I felt ashamed for sharing intimate space with my sister, whom I normally loved hanging out with, especially before going to sleep. We would laugh uncontrollably in the dark, forcing our tired, annoyed mother to barge into the room and tell us to go to sleep. But after the boy called me a sissy, sleeping in the same bed with my sister meant something very different. I didn't want to be anyone's sissy, whatever that was. I grew to resent having to sleep in the same bed with her. My brief encounter with this boy made me self-conscious about my public image around other boys and men. Growing up male, encounters like this happened throughout my life, all the way through adulthood. I'm no different than most men—I have been guilty of feminizing other men, too. I've referred to other males on the football field as "pussies," and accused dudes on the basketball court of making a "bitch call" when they called weak fouls. I demeaned my fraternity brothers by calling them "cat" if they did not conform to the codes of manhood as defined by the fraternity.

My first experience with violence, at age five, forever shattered my boyhood openness and trust around unfamiliar boys. It also taught me one of my first lessons about manhood. One Saturday afternoon, while playing alone in my front yard near my favorite red maple tree, I was approached by a slightly older boy. "Do you know where 58 Acorn Avenue is?" he asked. A little confused, I asked him to repeat himself. He moved in closer, about an arm's length away, and asked again: *"Do you know where 58 Acorn Avenue is?"* I became excited because I knew the answer to his question. "It's right *here!*" I said, bright with naïveté, pointing to my house. Before I knew it, and without provocation, the boy swung and punched me hard in my right eye, and ran away.

I could not believe what was happening to me. Of course I was shocked and felt tremendous pain, but more than that, I was stricken with fear and confusion. I ran into the house, screaming and crying to my father, who lay on the couch asleep. My wailing woke him up, and I leaped into his arms for comfort. But rather than consoling me or attending to my rapidly swelling eye, he put on his brown slippers and took me to our car. He told me to point in the direction the older boy ran, and with my only remaining eye open, I showed him the last place I saw him go.

We spent what seemed like hours driving around the neighborhood looking for the boy. My father was dead set on finding him so that I could confront and fight him. But truth be told, I wanted no part of that crazy boy. I was absolutely terrified at the thought of having to face him again. Had I known that my father would use this as a "rite of passage" opportunity for me to "prove my manhood," I would have gone to my mother, who surely would have had me lying in bed with an ice pack over my eye, and maybe some ice cream, too. Instead, my pops took me on a search-and-destroy mission. Luckily, we never found that boy, but the memory remains fresh in my mind.

My father's lesson to me that day was clear. His uncompromising stance signaled to me that he "didn't want to raise no punk." His moral lesson in driving around to look for the boy was to *never* let anybody push you around without retaliating. A boy who didn't fight back was no boy at all. Like most men, I think my father was taught that manhood is a nonnegotiable currency, and any sign of weakness makes you a walking target to other boys. In essence, I think my pops was trying to induct his son into the world of patriarchy—a social system that says males are supposed to dominate, to reign superior over everyone who appears weak, especially girls and women, and maintain that dominance and rule through fear and violence if necessary. He wanted to teach his son an early lesson on surviving on the street—or rather, surviving in the world of violent masculinity.

Later in life, while my father worked two jobs and battled alcohol dependency, my boys around the way replaced him as my models of male identity. They taught me similar lessons about how to negotiate conflict with other guys. I learned that my "manhood" rested on my ability to handle myself physically. My friends and I practiced the art of slap-boxing for hours at a time. This was to prepare us for the "real deal"—fighting in the street, at school, at the bus stop, at the movies, and at parties. I always hated to fight, but did so often just to prove to my male friends (and occasionally to girls as well) that I was not a sucker. My mother had a very different approach. She was a kind and gentle woman who didn't want me to solve problems by fighting. Instead of my father's "hit 'em first and hit 'em hard" philosophy, my mom encouraged me to "talk things through" whenever I had a conflict with dudes at school. I found her approach laughable for the simple fact that it was wholly unrealistic to me. Noble as it was, and as much as I *wanted* to avoid getting into fights, "talking it through" had severe consequences. It meant that you were too scared to fight, and couldn't hold your own. It meant, in essence, that you were "a soft nigga," which was about the worst thing you could ever be considered among Black males. At that stage of my life, backing down from senseless confrontation was somehow unacceptable. I remember feeling trapped by this code of the street, knowing it was messed up. But male peer culture allowed no space for diplomacy. So I rolled with it, honing my slap-boxing skills on the corner daily with my friends Greg, Peanut, and Chris. To this day, I still feel equipped to handle myself physically. I'll slap-box the *crap* out of you if the situation calls for it, but if the guns come out, well, then I have a real problem on my hands. As cultural critic bell hooks points out in her book *The Will to Change: Men, Masculinity and Love,* "The most passive, kind, quiet man can come to violence if the seeds of patriarchal thinking have been embedded in his psyche."

The seeds of typical American maleness have been planted in my psyche, and even though I am no longer a violent person (I haven't had a fight in at least fifteen years), with enough provocation, my ability to become violent is there at a moment's notice. All my life I've been well trained to be a violent man, and in moments of anger or frustration I constantly have to remind myself not to use violence to express my emotions. Even though I'm not a violent person, I still have urges to use violence when I get angry. I've learned to de-escalate my rage and talk myself out of situations where I feel like using violence against another person.

Because I am a child of the 1970s and the early 1980s, media played its role in shaping my male identity. On big and small screens alike, stoic, tough-guy characters were the norm. Particularly beloved by my father's generation were 1950s and '60s westerns like John Wayne in *The Searchers* and Chuck Connors in *The Rifleman.* Then there were the macho 1970s "Blaxploitation" actors like Richard Roundtree as *Shaft* and Ron O'Neal as Super Fly, not to mention 1970s and '80s kung-fu stars like Bruce Lee in *Fists of Fury* and Jackie Chan in *Drunken Master*. The 1980s and '90s brought new action movie megastars like Sylvester Stallone in *Rambo*, Arnold Schwarzenegger in *The Terminator*, and Bruce Willis in *Die Hard*. Such were my cinematic examples of "manly men."

As boys, my friends and I loved kung-fu flicks and action movies. We bought into these glamorized media images because they appealed to our budding manhood. These action heroes also seemed to be respected by other men. Through their onscreen bravado, these male characters taught us to be tough and invulnerable, to repress our emotions (except anger), and to associate manhood with aggression and violence. The best among these "rugged individuals" always got the beautiful woman (or women), which only inspired us to emulate what we saw on the screen.

My views on manhood were also influenced by rap music and hiphop culture. In the early to mid-1970s the emergence of rap music took New York City and its surrounding areas by storm. Ever since rap's infancy, young people from my hometown, Central Islip (C.I.), Long Island, were hyped to get into the rap game. C.I. has produced several rap artists including the JVC Force (*Strong Island*), K-Solo (*Your Mom's in My Business*), and Keith Murray (*The Most Beautifullest Thing*). Rapper Biz Markie ("The Vapors") could be found walking the streets of Central Islip, where he performed at many backyard parties. EPMD (*You Gots to Chill*) and Craig Mack ("Flava in Ya Ear") were also from around my way. To associate in any way with Long Island rappers that we knew personally or felt connected to, made us feel proud to be a significant part of hiphop culture. For the most part, though, guys from Long Island were considered "soft" in comparison to guys from any of the five boroughs of New York City.

The JVC Force's *Strong Island* (a term coined by legendary rapper Chuck D of Public Enemy) gave Long Island guys a stronger, more masculine identity within New York City's hierarchy. Groups like Eric B. & Rakim, Public Enemy, Busta Rhymes's Leaders of the New School, and De La Soul gave us an added boost.

The first rap song I ever heard was "Supersperm" by Captain Sky. My older neighbors Darryl and Herbie blasted the song repeatedly on their sound system, and it blared through their open windows in the summertime. At that time, I didn't know what rap music was or what "Supersperm" was about, but I loved it. Rap music soon became the soundtrack to my life as hiphop culture took hold of my generation. I didn't just listen to rap, I wanted to *be* a rapper. During football camp in my sophomore year in high school, the "rookies" had to perform skits for the "veterans." My friend Jeff Ford and I chose to perform "The Show" by Slick Rick and Doug E. Fresh. When the beat dropped, the older players on the team shouted, "*Ohhhhhhhhhh!!!*" and started waving their arms from side to side. Our skit was a major hit, and to this day, every time I hear "The Show" I think about our performance.

Jeff and I grew to be close friends. We would spend hours down in his basement listening to rap music. Jeff practiced cutting, scratching, and mixing records on his turntables, and I tried writing rhymes. He was an excellent DJ and he went on to pursue a career in the rap game. But I was horrible at writing rhymes. I just couldn't commit to writing a full song, and eventually gave up trying. I also tried my hand at breakdancing and pop-locking, joining a small crew called Home Boys Only (HBO). But I wasn't any good at breaking or popping, and HBO dissolved within weeks. My gift was for throwing a football, so I stuck with quarterbacking and remained a loyal hiphop fan.

Although rap started out mainly as party music, it evolved and took on other forms. Unfortunately, the more popular rap music became with White audiences, the more limited the lyrics became. Young Black and Latino male rappers increasingly rhymed about stereotypical themes of sexual prowess, drug use, and criminality. Rap lyrics digressed from party time and pro-black upliftment to recurrent gun talk, materialism, misogyny, and homophobia. Such narrow depictions of Black manhood further cemented racist stereotypes that Black and brown males are dangerous, oversexed, immoral, and disrespectful.

Corporate executives have consistently rewarded artists for presenting these negative themes, and successfully marginalized the more threatening and challenging Black male rappers who've offered more progressive, socially conscious, and political lyrics—thus making it more enticing for young Black males to pursue a "gangsta" rap image over the less commercially viable "conscious rapper" mode. During the Reagan and Bush administrations in the 1980s and early '90s, crack cocaine flooded poor and working-class neighborhoods as drug addiction reached epidemic proportions, devastating Black families and communities. As a result, hiphop grew edgier, more violent and crass, and reflected the grit of street life.

Though it's often used as a scapegoat, hiphop is rarely given credit for its nuance and complexity. Hiphop purists understand that hiphop is not monolithic, but to the casual hiphop fan, the dominant images in mainstream hiphop perpetuate very limited ideas about manhood. As a Black man who speaks to young men of color at high schools, youth groups, and college campuses throughout the world, I can clearly see the impact these images are having on us collectively. Many Black males believe that their path to success in life leads through hiphop. As a result, they mimic what they see and hear on corporate rap stations.

This represents a tragic state of affairs. Although hiphop has been called rebellious, revolutionary, and subversive to America's status quo, some of the most regressive values about American manhood can be found on commercial hiphop stations and in music videos.

My award-winning documentary film, *Hip-Hop: Beyond Beats and Rhymes,* examines this reality. In 2000, I was watching the rap music video countdown on BET's *Rap City* when I noticed that almost every video appeared to be exactly the same. They all featured dudes throwing money at the camera, dudes in fancy cars showing off their "iced-out" jewelry and, of course, lots of scantily dressed, sexually available women as background props.

As I saw how formulaic rap music videos had become, I began to wonder, How do Black men feel about the representations of manhood in hiphop culture? How do Black women and men feel about the pervasive images of sexually objectified women in rap music videos? How do Black males truly feel about the way women and violence are talked about in rap music? What do today's rap lyrics tell us about the collective consciousness of Black males and females from the hiphop generation? What does homoeroticism in hiphop media look like? I decided to pick up the camera to make a film about the gender politics of the music and the culture that I grew up with and loved.

Hiphop culture spoke to me so loudly as a young male because its chief storytellers were like me: young, Black and Brown. But it also resonated with me because most of the images were so deeply masculine. Hardcore hiphop has strong masculine energy. To this day, when I listen to it—whether alone, with friends, or working out at the gym—it makes me feel emboldened and powerful. I'll never forget riding to practices, parties, and the movies in a car packed full of my teammates and friends, listening to hiphop. It felt *cool* and *rugged* to be in a posse full of guys, blastin' beats. I spent many Saturday afternoons in the locker room with my earphones on, listening to hard-core gangster rap and getting jacked up for a big football game.

But hiphop cannot take all the credit or the blame for shaping my masculine identity. Even more powerful was the omnipresent influence of American popular culture that teaches boys how to be men. Heaping too much criticism on hiphop is both intellectually dishonest and racist. To deflect the criticism onto rap music is to disproportionately blame Black and Latino males while giving White males a pass.

In April 2007, when radio and television talk show host Don Imus infamously referred to the Rutgers women's basketball team as "nappy-headed hos," he later claimed to be criticizing hiphop culture. But hiphop only reinforced the lesson I learned elsewhere in the culture about manhood. Had hiphop never been created in the early 1970s, violence, sexism, and homophobia would still pervade our popular culture. Harvard President Lawrence Summers's remark during a conference on women and science says all you need to know about the sexism ingrained in academia: "Women are not genetically well equipped to handle the sciences."

Nor does hiphop explain why NBA star Tim Hardaway would tell a Miami sports radio station, "You know I hate gay people, so I let it be known, I am homophobic. I don't like gay people and I don't like to be around gay people. I am homophobic. I don't like it. It shouldn't be in the world or in the United States."

Patriarchal values about money, sex, crass materialism, power, domination, homophobia, sexism, misogyny, and egotism are everywhere you look in the United States. One look at actor Robert De Niro's body of work will prove that. His films are filled with hyperaggressive images, as are the films of Al Pacino, Schwarzenegger, Vin Diesel, Jean-Claude Van Damme, Roger Moore, Sean Connery, Charles Bronson, Clint Eastwood, Sylvester Stallone, Mel

Gibson, Harrison Ford, Bruce Willis, Jet Li, and countless others. Yet these male actors are upheld in society and considered to be the greatest entertainers of our generation. Schwarzenegger was even elected governor of California. Despite hiphop's "keepin' it real" mantra, most men in hiphop are *performing* the same sort of exaggerated masculinity as these A-list Hollywood stars. Rappers and actors are well paid by huge multinational corporations to perpetuate hypermasculinity, not to redefine manhood.

Through all these cultural influences—sports, family, media, and military culture—the messages sent to us about boyhood and manhood are loud and clear: boys and men are better than girls and women, boys and men do not cry, boys and men are tough and strong, and boys and men are violent and aggressive. After years of this rigid training, I cultivated a pretty convincing macho image. Nobody could question my masculine credentials. In high school I was an "All–Long Island" quarterback on the football team, our school's homecoming and prom king, and an above-average shooting guard on the basketball team who was hugely popular and respected. By the time I was a senior in high school, I was every preadolescent boy's dream: a highly recruited stand-out quarterback, and a good student who was popular with girls, and socially accepted. Everyone around me—students, teachers, guidance counselors, principals, family, and my local community members—conferred that status upon me, and I wholeheartedly embraced it. I was, by most accounts, "The Man."

As I moved on to my college years at Northeastern University, I began to think seriously about my future. As a scholarship student-athlete, I wanted to take full advantage of a university that planned to exploit my athletic ability. As a freshman, I made the dean's list, and made an effort to be heavily involved in student activities. My African American Studies courses enriched my college experience, but disturbed my coaches. One day before football practice, I was in my coach's office and we were going over new plays to be installed for an upcoming game, when he looked down and saw my course schedule for the next quarter. He noticed my classes, "Intro to African American Studies" and "Black Man/Black Woman." He looked up at me and said to me, "What is this?" Matter-of-factly I replied, "Oh, I had two electives open this quarter so I decided to take these two." "So, why are you taking *these* classes?" he asked. I felt a need to defend my desire to explore Black history. "Because I'm interested in African American culture," I replied. Then he asked me a question that completely caught me off guard: "What are you here for, *to get an education, or to play football?*" At first I thought he was joking. Northeastern is not a football powerhouse like Michigan or Ohio State, and my chances of going pro were slim. Surely he had to be kidding. But when I looked at his face, I could tell he was dead serious. I paused for a second, because I didn't know if it was a trick question or not. "Both," I said. He looked at me speechless, and that was the end of the conversation. He felt he had a militant Black quarterback on his hands.

I wanted to destroy the notion that Black athletes were only on campus to play sports. During my five years at Northeastern University (NU offers a five-year cooperative education program where you can alternate course work with job experience in your field of study) I was, among other things, co-editor of the Black student newspaper, DJ on the campus radio station, and a first-place winner of the Dean Roland E. Latham oratory competition, sponsored by the John D. O'Bryant African-American Institute. I am most proud of winning the Nguzo Saba Award, which is given to Black students who exemplify the seven principles of Kwanzaa. Perhaps the least significant of my accomplishments was winning the Most Promising Athlete award. In addition to excelling on campus, as a co-op student I interned at three major television stations in Boston, and was a student beat reporter for the *Patriot Ledger* in Quincy. I also pledged a historically Black fraternity, Omega Psi Phi.

I was smart, determined, ambitious, and focused. Like most men, I wanted to acquire status, money, and material things. I wanted to become a functional part of the dominant (read: White) society, and achieve institutional access and upward mobility. I figured my life would be complete if I could have a nice house, a dope car, a beautiful wife, and a high-profile position at a successful company. That would definitely make me a man, right? But I soon learned that complete access into corporate America was not a guarantee, especially as a Black male in America. Plain and simple, it's much more difficult for a Black man to find a job than it is for a White man. When you look at the grim reality of unemployment for Black men, the model of "male breadwinner" does not necessarily apply. Especially when you consider that in 2004, fifty percent of Black men in their twenties were jobless in New York City, up from 46 percent in 2000. Are those unemployed Black males not men because they don't have jobs? So why should manhood be based on one's ability to have and keep a job or make more money than women?

Our system of patriarchy leaves little room for career hardship or economic failure for Black males. Your "manhood" will be questioned in ways similar to how it would be questioned if you backed down from physical confrontation. I have been thinking about these issues surrounding manhood for years. They are the reason why I have chosen to divest, as best I can, from definitions of manhood that really do not empower me at the end of the day. And what gave me the tools to divest from these rigid rules? I had a very important intervention—a sheer twist of fate— that would alter my life plan and forever change my perspective on manhood.

In August 1993, as I was about to graduate from Northeastern, my former athletic academic advisor, Keith McDermott, told me about a new job opening at Northeastern's Center for the Study of Sport in Society (CSSS). Founded by Richard Lapchick in 1984, CSSS is the world's leading social justice organization using sport to create social change. Keith didn't know much about this new program, called Mentors in Violence Prevention (MVP), but he thought I might be interested. As a student-athlete, I had given talks to students in the Boston school system about violence prevention, avoiding drug use, and the value of education. I enjoyed this sort of community outreach because I liked to believe I was making a small difference by giving back. So when I heard the creator of the MVP program was looking for a former athlete to fill the position, I thought it could be a good match. I graduated with a degree in journalism, but I wanted to make a difference in the lives of young people. I thought this job with MVP might be a good *temporary* gig until I got a "real" job working in television broadcasting. I sent my résumé over to CSSS and got called back for an interview. Days later, I went over to CSSS for an interview with Jackson Katz, the White Jewish former football standout turned antisexist activist, who was the visionary behind the program.

During the interview, Jackson told me that the MVP program was a *gender* violence prevention program, not just a *violence* prevention program. He told me he was looking for a male athlete with the leadership qualities, courage, and passion to challenge and inspire men to speak out against sexism and violence against women. The job would entail teaching men proactive skills to prevent abusive behavior before it happened. Two questions immediately popped into my head: *How did I get into this man's office again?* And: *How am I going to get myself out of here without it being too obvious that I'm not interested?* Behind those, other questions lurked: *If I take this job, what will my ex-teammates, fraternity brothers, father, uncles, and cousins think of me? Would they think I was soft or weak, a traitor, or too "sensitive?"* Twenty-three years of social conditioning rushed over me. The worst of all my fears was the thought that guys would think I was gay if I took the job. I felt overwhelmed, like I was having an out-of-body experience. Physically, I was still there in the office with Jackson, but mentally, I was somewhere in outer space. Then, just as I was about to completely check out, Jackson asked me two questions I will never forget.

"Byron, do you consider yourself to be a leader?" he asked. That was an easy one for me to answer. I had been an athlete for most of my life. For fifteen years I played quarterback—a leadership position—and I held leadership positions throughout high school and college. "Yes, I do," I answered. He explained how so few men were willing to risk their masculine credibility by speaking out against sexism and violence against women. Appealing to my leadership sensibilities, he told me how much of a difference I could make by educating myself about gender, and using my voice to speak out against male abusive behavior. Because of my masculine credibility, he told me other men would listen to what I had to say.

Then he asked me another provocative question: "Byron, how does Black men's sexism and violence toward Black women uplift Black people?" No one, Black, White, male or female, had ever posed such a question to me. I thought for a minute, then replied, simply, "It doesn't." There was no other logical response. Jackson began to explain how racial and gender oppression were interconnected and how this job was about ending gender and sexual violence in general, and helping Black people by eradicating an age-old problem in the African American community. This pulled me back in. By the time he invited me to attend a workshop the next day on campus, I was already intrigued.

The workshop was mixed-race and mixed-gender. Jackson quickly defined the issue by breaking down just how pervasive male violence against women is in the United States. "Men murder four women per day in the United States," he said. "Battering is the leading cause of injury to young women in America—more than rape, muggings, and automobile accidents combined." Then he got interactive: "If battering is the leading cause of injury to girls and women in the United States," he asked, "then who is doing the battering?" We replied in unison: "*Men.*"

Then he took us through an exercise that blew me away. Using a black marker, Jackson drew the Greek symbol representing "man" on one easel, and the symbol representing "woman" on another easel. He asked the men in the room the following question: "Men, what things do you do on a daily basis to protect yourself from being raped or sexually assaulted?" I looked around the room at the other men, wondering if they knew something I didn't. After some nervous laughter, one man finally raised his hand and said, "Nothing." "Thank you," Jackson said. Continuing with the exercise, he asked the women in the room the same question: "What things do you do on a daily basis to protect yourself from being raped or sexually assaulted?" Immediately, several women raised their hand. One by one, women from various racial backgrounds rattled off all the ways they tried to protect themselves:

I don't walk alone at night. I look underneath my car before I get in. I walk with my keys in between my fingers, so I can use my keys as a weapon. I don't jog by myself at night. When I jog alone, I jog with my dog. I don't live in first-floor apartments. I don't put my drink down at clubs or parties. I use the buddy system when I go out. I leave a male voice on my home voice mail. I don't put my first name in the phone book. I take self-defense courses. I cross the street when I see a group of young men walking toward me. I carry mace or pepper spray. I don't get in an elevator with a group of men I don't know. I park in well-lit parking areas.

The list went on and on.

I was floored. Juxtaposed with the endless list of precautions females were taking, the male easel was blank. I couldn't believe women had to do all of these things on a daily basis. Suddenly I realized that there were a lot of things about women's lives that I did not know and understand. I thought about my mother, my sister, my aunts, and girlfriends both past and present. I thought about my own history of being verbally and emotionally abusive, as well as my failure to confront sexist behavior in others. I thought about my father and his emotional abuse toward my mother. I thought about all the ways I've seen men mistreat women. There was no denying that this was a real issue.

Listening to the women tell their stories, and hearing Jackson talk passionately about the need for men to change the peer climate that makes gender and sexual violence socially acceptable, had a major impact on me. I went home that night and talked to my parents about the job interview. I told them that I wanted to try it out. My mother was pleased that I had a job offer, but my father seemed reticent. "Are you qualified for this job?" he asked.

I assured him that I was, and that I had made up my mind. The next day, I accepted the job as a mentor-training specialist, signing on for one year at an $18,000 salary—clearly, I didn't accept the job for the money.

And that's how I became an antisexist activist. It was one of the best decisions I've made in my life. Over the past fifteen years I have learned so much about men, women, and myself. I've expanded my awareness of social justice to include gender oppression *as well as* racial and class oppression. I have challenged my own attitudes about women, and I am more open to receive constructive criticism from women about the remnants of my sexism. At thirty-eight years old, I have found my voice. I am confident in speaking out about male privilege and all forms of gender violence. Most importantly, I have made an indelible impact on the lives of men and women across race, class, and gender lines. I feel healthier today than I did prior to 1993, and I know I am making a positive contribution to the world.

None of my ideas about masculinity are original. I became gender conscious with the help and support of many people—female and male—who were more knowledgeable than I about gender issues. Through these brilliant people, I learned that I had been conditioned to be sexist, and that my abusive behavior was a by-product of this conditioning. I also learned that even as a Black male with no real institutional power, I benefited from male privilege. I began to think critically about my upbringing and the larger social and political system of patriarchal masculinity in ways that most men do not. Challenging my own sexism and male privilege has been a long and painstaking process. Inspiring other men to do the same kind of introspective work has also been very challenging. But it is necessary and gratifying work. Although I was initially reluctant to accept the challenge of confronting male sexism and violence against women for fear of what other men would think of me, I am very happy that I decided to rise above my fears. There have been countless moments when I wanted to take the easy way out, and quit, leaving gender and sexual violence prevention work for women and other men to do. But I now understand that educating the world about gender issues is what I was born to do. This is my calling, and I embrace it with purpose and passion. I am happy to say that I have been able to address tens of thousands of boys and men around the world, spreading the message of redefining manhood.

As a filmmaker and activist, my goal is to push people's awareness around race, class, and gender issues. This is an ambitious goal, because the system of patriarchy is deeply entrenched and interwoven into the fabric of our culture. More and more people are coming to understand how gender and sexual violence hurt women. Too few understand how it hurts men. Several years ago I facilitated a workshop on men's violence against women on a Marine Corps base in Hawaii. During the workshop, two Marines—one Black, the other White—acknowledged growing up in homes where their fathers physically assaulted their mothers. As they shared their stories, both men became very emotional. They described how painful it was for them to watch their fathers beat their mothers. They expressed how powerless they felt, and how much their childhood experience with domestic violence affected them in their own relationships with women. Both men broke down and cried as they told their stories. It became clear to me in that moment how men's abusive behavior hurts males as well as females.

The workshop, facilitated by men, gave the men in the room an opportunity, a safe space in which to talk about manhood and violence against women. Men need other men to give them the space to talk about being a man in a culture where patriarchy thwarts our ability to talk about our painful experiences, and suppresses our humanity. Just how Ernie Simpson's status and masculine credibility influenced dozens of boys in my neighborhood to sign up for the Pop Warner football program thirty-one years ago, I hope to use mine to influence boys and men throughout the world to sign up to be on our team—working to redefine what it means to be a man.

My dad died from pancreatic cancer on June 23, 2007. It was a devastating loss for my family and me. We lost a patriarch, a spiritual leader, and a devoted family man. I would have done *anything* to save my father's life. I would have given him my own pancreas—even cut off my right arm—if I could spend another day with him in the flesh, just to have a conversation about the race and gender dynamics in the 2008 presidential election. I wish he were here to witness the brilliance of Barack Obama, a Black man so close to capturing the White House. Despite the typical father/son strife during my teenage years, my father and I were very close, especially toward the end of his life. He always supported me, encouraging me to grow, spread my wings, set big goals, and live my dreams. We would go to lunch together, talk about politics, and race and culture. He had the kind of intellectual hardware I long to have, and he shared his wisdom with me without being preachy. He looked forward to being a grandfather and watching my wife and me raise a family. My father was a bull of a man, spiritually mature, and not easily defeated. He battled pancreatic cancer—a disease that wreaks havoc on the body and takes lives in a matter of months—for three years. He saw my film *Hip-Hop: Beyond Beats and Rhymes* premiere at the Sundance Film Festival, and we watched it air nationally on PBS as a family, in the hospital on Long Island in New York. Although my father was very conscious of race, things like sexism and violence against women were not priorities for him. I don't think he ever really critically examined his own sexism and male privilege. I do think my own examination of gender issues challenged him. I could tell that his attitudes around gender issues were evolving. A couple of years before he died, he began to wear a baseball cap that I gave him, which read *A Call To Men: End Violence Against Women*. That was a huge step for him. He would have never publicly worn that hat if his son were not an antisexist activist.

Before he died, he told me everything a father should tell his son: that he loved me, that he was proud of me, and that my life was "about something." Nothing meant more to me than to hear him say that. I loved him so much, and I think about him every single day. I think about him before I go to bed at night, and I wake up in the morning thinking about the contributions he made, shaping my life, my world, and my cultural identity. I wish more men had the opportunity to get to know a father so committed to raising a son. He was not a perfect man. He had flaws and contradictions just like you and me. But he was a strong Black man who endured the brutal stereotypes, racist assaults, and limited opportunities faced by many men of his generation. He did for me what his father could and did not do for him: love and nurture his son well into adulthood.

Like many men who grew up in his era, my father struggled to deal with his emotions in a healthy way. An intellect, he showed his love by sharing his head, not his heart. Revealing flaws and weaknesses was never his thing. I think he thought it would diminish his manhood. But as his son, I often yearned for him to share his ideas about race and culture, and show me his vulnerable side. I wish that my father had felt more comfortable sharing some of his insecurities, self-doubts, and fears about being a *man*—not just being a Black man. I think it would have helped me develop more quickly into the healthy man that I am today. But for a young Black male reared in the Deep South, during an era where White supremacy and patriarchy was a form of domestic terrorism, my father did the absolute best he could for his family. I know that deep in my heart. His love, his brilliance, his sacrifice, his struggles, his pain, his knowledge, and wisdom carry me as I make choices in life as a human being on this earth. He's with me all the time in spirit, teaching me powerful lessons. Although I miss his physical presence greatly, I know I'll be seeing him tonight as soon as I close my eyes.

So here are five things that I have done on my journey to become more aware about race, class, and gender issues. To become a wiser, better whole being. To become a man. I hope you can find some of these tactics useful in your own process of redefining and claiming your manhood:

1. *Find a mentor.* Choose a family member, a teacher, a professor, a coach, someone in your professional field, or someone in your community who is knowledgeable about race and culture. Learn from him or her, and do not be intimidated to ask questions. Older, established people often love to share their knowledge and expertise when asked. Overcome your fears about approaching an older person, and ask them to be your mentor.

2. *Read strategically.* Reading helps you to expand your mind and develop your consciousness. Reading also strengthens your vocabulary and sharpens

your critical thinking skills. Please go to my website, www.bhurt.com, for a suggested reading list.

3. *Be self-reflective.* Think deeply about your own life experiences and the choices that you've made. Be honest about your strengths and weaknesses and commit to becoming a better, healthier man. Keep yourself open to constructive criticism. Do not get defensive when people challenge you about your flaws or "issues." Use criticism as a way to grow.

4. *Honor yourself.* Give yourself your own best advice and listen to your instincts. Be who you are and don't just conform to what others think you should be. Trust that you know what's right for yourself, your family, and your loved ones.

5. *Use your voice.* Speak up when you see racist, sexist, or homophobic behavior. Do not remain silent in the face of male abuse. Be creative and strategic about how to confront them. Protect yourself from getting in harm's way, but make sure you do something as opposed to doing nothing at all.

4

Starting A Plan for Economic Empowerment
By Ryan Mack

IMMEDIATE ATTENTION

A father wakes up at 3:00 AM to a crying baby. He runs into the other room to see what is wrong and rocks the baby back to sleep. But what will happen if the father doesn't answer the baby's cry?

A father sees his son fall from a tree and break his arm. Without thinking he picks him up and rushes him to the hospital for treatment. What will happen if the father doesn't take his child to the hospital?

The possible answers to these questions are so unbearable that both individuals are forced to take action. Faced with such an urgent situation, most individuals' reactions are a matter of instinct. Failure to respond could bring drastic results. Whatever else might have seemed important at the time, we put it aside to attend to the situation that has arisen.

My Black brothers—especially the black teenagers and young adults reading this essay—we have a drastic situation on our hands that demands our immediate attention. No matter what stage of life you are currently in, we all must find a way to learn financial literacy and apply the principles of economic empowerment within our lives. What are you doing that is so important that you can't find the time to learn how to apply these important life skills? Perhaps you don't perceive your financial future as urgent. Consider these facts:

- By their sixty-fifth birthday, 93 percent of Americans require the financial support of family and friends or Social Security *just to provide for basic necessities.* (U.S. Department of Labor)
- Fewer men are worth $100 at age sixty-eight after fifty years of hard work, than at age eighteen. (Denby's Economic Tables)
- Eighty-five percent of all people have *only $250 in cash at retirement.* (Social Security Administration)
- Over one-third of all Black senior citizens *live below the poverty level* as established by the federal government. (U.S. Census)
- Two and a quarter million senior citizens forfeit their Social Security because *they have to work.* (Social Security Administration)

There are two types of people in this world: those who are proactive and those who are reactive. The reactive person lives his or her life by responding to changes as they come. The proactive person lives his or her life by preparing for what could occur in advance, and making his or her decisions appropriately. As a people we can no longer afford to keep responding to problems that have been plaguing our race for hundreds of years. We owe it to ourselves and to future generations to be proactive enough to embrace principles of fiscal responsibility as a steadfast component of our daily lives.

Financial literacy is a relatively new language to Black males in the United States, and it can be very intimidating for those who are unfamiliar with its complexities. I urge you all to be patient, as there is no such thing as a "quick-fix" to our current economic situation. However, as you begin to embrace and apply these principles, you will begin to see changes not only in your life, but in the lives of loved ones in your community.

Over these next few pages I will attempt to explain various aspects of financial literacy to introduce you to this very important concept. I emphasize "introduce" because reading this is only the beginning of a very long journey. Learning about economic empowerment principles is only half the battle. You must also apply these principles in your daily living for the sake of your community, your family, and yourself. Knowledge by itself is useless, but knowledge plus action is power. I urge all of you, upon reading this book, to aggressively take positive action.

ARE YOU STILL A SLAVE?

Slavery is not only a physical state but also a mental state. Any Black male who carries the notion that he lacks the ability to attain economic prosperity within himself, or who feels as if he must rely upon the decisions and influence of others who hold the key to his financial future, is still a slave. Let me explain the concept of slavery as it relates to economic independence and financial empowerment.

The Black male comes from a strong bloodline of prosperity

within a rich ancient ancestry. However, here in the United States, an oppressive society has been successful in creating the overwhelmingly popular, inaccurate perception within the Black male that he is incapable of creating his own economic reality—that he is incapable of achieving financial independence. It is unfortunate but true that many of us allow ourselves to believe this and therefore allow an oppressive society to control our lives and shape our destinies. If it is true that the next phase of the civil rights movement will be fought on an economic front, it is imperative that the Black male free himself from this form of mental slavery that prevents him from achieving economic independence.

Are you a slave? This is a question all Black males must ask themselves before they can understand the critical importance of financial empowerment, and certainly before they can effectively contribute to the advancement of the Black race. Let's examine the definition of the word *slavery:*

The American Heritage Dictionary defines slavery as:

1. The state of one bound in servitude as the property of a slaveholder or household.
2. The condition of being subject to a specified influence.
3. The state of being under control of another person.

The first definition describes a "physical" state in which someone is physically bound and held as a piece of property. The second and third definitions are not necessarily a physical state of being, but can also describe a mental state. If I allow you to influence or keep me under your control without any physical constraints or boundaries, then the control and influence must be mental. In essence, if I allow others to control me and/or my destiny, then I am still a slave.

So are you a slave? Below is a series of questions that you can answer to assist you in determining if your mentality is that of a slave or if you have taken the all-important first step to financial freedom by breaking the mental chains of bondage.

1. Oppression, racism, and discrimination are substantial obstacles to overcome and have understandably resulted in the lack of financial success for many Black males. Is it possible for a Black man to overcome these obstacles and be successful? ❑ Yes ❑ No

2. Is it possible for someone who comes from an inner-city neighborhood to be successful without government and/or family support? ❑ Yes ❑ No

3. Ward Connerly of the American Civil Rights Institute is attempting to end affirmative action, deeming it unconstitutional and racist. If this effort is successful will it be possible for Blacks to be successful? ❑ Yes ❑ No

4. If you lost your job tomorrow, would you be able to find a legal way to financially support yourself and your family? ❑ Yes ❑ No

5. If a hurricane demolished your home and left your family homeless, would it be possible for you and your family to recover? ❑ Yes ❑ No

All five questions describe real-life scenarios that have already been experienced by thousands and could happen to you in the very near future. If you did not answer "Yes" to all of the above questions, then you are under the control of your environment. You too are a slave.

However, if you answered "Yes" to all the questions, you should prepare yourself for a life of abundance. Having broken the mental chains of slavery, your destiny will be as fruitful and expansive as you desire it to be. Your thoughts determine your words, which determine your actions, which determine your habits, which determine your character, which determines your destiny.

BLACK MALES' FINANCIAL LEGACY

Let's go back to *The American Heritage Dictionary* for a definition of *legacy:*

1. Money or property bequeathed to another by will.
2. Something handed down from an ancestor or a predecessor from the past.

African Americans have long been disadvantaged because of the circumstances that brought us to America. Immigrants came to this land with their cultures intact and with strong self-esteem, both of which resulted in a strong entrepreneurial spirit. Slaves, by contrast, were broken down emotionally as well as physically, and were denied the same opportunities for many years.

Even after emancipation, our oppression continued. We were not afforded equal opportunities to advance professionally and to control our own businesses. For example, the radio was invented in the early 1900s and soon found its way into the homes of thousands of Americans. Shortly thereafter, the government disseminated the broadcast rights to an exclusive list comprising the most affluent in society. Similar milestones in television and other broadcasting networks have resulted in many families leaving strong legacies, adding to a foundation of wealth and prosperity that stretches back to the days of America's founding fathers. African Americans did not have an opportunity to own radio stations until WERD in Atlanta began broadcasting in the late 1940s.

It is indeed true that Black people have not had the best of opportunities since arriving in this country. In fact, we continue to face many forms of degradation and discrimination. However, even with the strife that we have endured, we are at a point where we need to take accountability for our own actions. In many ways, we continue to be the cause of the inhibition of our own economic growth.

Most of us did not receive an inheritance to give us a solid foundation of wealth and prosperity. But we may fail to realize that "eighty percent of America's millionaires are first-generation rich." (According to *The Millionaire Next Door*, by Thomas Stanley and William Danko.) Many of us are still beset by difficult economic conditions. However, we must ask ourselves, What have we done with the little that we have? Have we continued to complain that it wasn't enough, or have we made the most of it and tried to increase what we do have?

IF NOT YOU, THEN WHO?

The plans of the diligent lead to profit as surely as haste leads to poverty.

—Proverbs 21:5

It is our obligation to take responsibility for whatever we have been given and continue to grow financially. The duty is ours alone, it is not the government's responsibility, and it certainly is not to be left to the same people in power who used discrimination to prevent our financial advancement. While affirmative action and welfare programs are still necessary, we must not use these systems as a crutch. Welfare was not intended as a sustainable means of living, only a temporary subsidy. The problem with relying on government programs to save us is that the government can only take people out of poverty. Our objective as Black males must be to take the mind-set of poverty out of the people.

Let's examine the statistics:

- Black unemployment rates are twice those of Whites.
- We own less than 3 percent of the wealth, even though we are 13 percent of the population.
- Forty-one percent of our households hold less than $1,000 in net worth.
- For every $100 Whites possess, Blacks possess between $8 and $19.
- The median Black family's net worth is $8,300 compared with the median White family's net worth of $56,000. (Figures are from *Black Wealth, White Wealth*, by Melvin Oliver and Thomas Shapiro.)

One might conclude that these discrepancies are the result of racism and the fact that most Blacks have not had access to a legacy of prosperity. However, of all the millionaires in America, "more than half never received as much as $1 in inheritance," according to *The Millionaire Next Door*, by Thomas Stanley and William Danko. In fact, "only 19% receive any income or wealth of any kind from a trust fund or an estate."

If African Americans want a piece of the pie, we must work

for it. What can we do to help ourselves? How can we turn these circumstances around and empower our own communities? The answer begins with yet another question: Why is it that 93 percent of our income is spent outside the community? Lee Jenkins, author of *Taking Care of Business*, wrote, "The Black dollar turns over less than once on an average before it leaves the Black community. Asians turn over their money nine times in their communities, and Whites turn their money over eight times before it leaves." Keeping money in our circle makes that circle stronger.

Money made within our communities should be spent for the benefit of the community. However, too many African Americans feel otherwise. Oftentimes we hear comments such as "You just can't work with Black people!" "Truth is—they are just too slow!" We have all heard such statements from other African Americans. As Dr. Martin Luther King, Jr., observed, "Whenever Pharaoh wanted to keep the slaves in slavery, he kept them fighting amongst themselves." Together we can do much more for ourselves than any one person can do.

Why are material things so important to us? Does a new car proclaim to the world that we have achieved financial success? Earl Graves, Jr., of *Black Enterprise* magazine, said, "Blacks on the average are six times more likely than Whites to buy a Mercedes, and the average income of a Black who buys a Jaguar is about one-third less than that of a White purchaser of the luxury vehicle."

There are those of us who can save to buy rims for our cars, but struggle to put our children through college. If I were to give you a stock tip to buy 10,000 shares of a stock at $2, and told you in advance that the stock would be worth $1.50 tomorrow, would you buy it? The obvious answer is "No." Then why do we spend so much of our money on things that can only go down in value? Many of us are going deeper into debt every day in order to buy assets that lose 25 percent or more of their value as soon as we take them from the vendor. Are you rich because you have a nice car? The typical millionaire has never spent more than $399 for a suit, $140 for a pair of shoes, or $235 for a wristwatch (again, according to *The Millionaire Next Door*). Is it so important to prove yourself to others that you are more concerned about your nice car or fancy watch than your children? It is our children who are suffering from this irresponsible behavior; it is our children and grandchildren who will be left without a legacy as a result of our excessive spending habits.

When I was in school, many of my friends, Black like me, attended school on borrowed money. But there were others who readily afforded college. I refer to them as the "trust fund babies," and as you can probably guess, few of them were Black. Parents of these "trust fund babies" began early to plan (and often to sacrifice) for their children's education early in life, while many African American parents were more concerned with what they were wearing and what car they were driving.

Why are some of us more concerned with material wealth than with establishing trust funds for our children? What inheritance is your child going to receive if you're forever increasing debt by spending money frivolously? Think about the superficial values and shallow desires glorified in videos and TV shows. Why is it so important to have a phat ride and a fancy house, champagne wishes and caviar dreams, gators on your feet and bling on your teeth, spinning wheels, rattling trunks? We as a people need to redefine our image of wealth. "He who works the land will have abundant food, but he who chases fantasies lacks judgment" (Proverbs 12:11).

When all is said and done, we have the ability to take control of our own destinies. Despite the racism our people have experienced, we have the capability to do for ourselves and achieve success. But first there must be a paradigm shift for African Americans, and specifically for Black males. It is our responsibility to build an inheritance, not just for ourselves, but for each of our own children and our communities. We must change our mind-set and think in terms of leaving legacies. "A good man leaveth an inheritance to his children's children." (Proverbs 13:22).

THE BLACK MALE VERSUS CONSUMPTION

Pick up that dictionary one more time and look up *consumption:*

1. The using up of goods having an exchangeable value.
2. The purchasing of goods that depreciate in value.

When the Black male participates in an act of consumption, he is not just spending money, he is using up goods that could have benefited his community, his family, and his own financial future. Blacks are spending over 90 percent of the Black dollar outside their own community and the majority of those funds are spent through consumption as opposed to savings, investment, or building Black-owned businesses. We must focus on creating more value with our hard-earned dollars, and that starts with limiting our impulse purchases. Consumption is not always easy to eliminate from our lives, so I have outlined some of the strategies that vendors use to separate you from your hard-earned dollars:

The Bogus Sale Strategy. Knowing that the majority of shoppers don't shop unless there is some kind of a special offer, producers will mark prices up then mark them down again and say the item is "on sale."

Example: A clothing store receives a jacket from the supplier. Normally this item would retail for $150, but the jacket's retail price is increased 100 percent to $300 because the clothing store recognizes that their (Black) customers will pay an inflated price due to the item's quality, trendiness, and overall popularity. If the jacket remains on the shelf for too long, the retailer will mark it down to $150 again and advertise a 50 percent "sale" in order to entice customers.

The "Guilt" Sales Strategy. Have you ever wondered why certain stores encourage you to try on as many clothes as possible? This is because many shoppers feel a sense of guilt after they have sampled many pieces of clothing, as if they are obligated to purchase something. Another method of creating guilt is serving light refreshments to the customer. Refreshments create customer loyalty, and also create a feeling of obligation to pay the store back by shopping.

The Impulse Creation Strategy. Stores have ways of creating a sense of urgency in their customers. One strategy is to limit the amount of supplies on the shelves. Many people try to be the first in line to buy that new pair of sneakers or that new gaming system because they believe the inventory will disappear quickly. The retailer wants to create a sense of panic so the customer will rush to purchase the item before the inventory is depleted. Another strategy is to rotate stock from one store to another to create the impression of limited supply. That fitted baseball cap seems much more valuable if it will only be on the shelf for another day or so.

If you feel that you are about to purchase an item on impulse, put it down for three days and think of all of the ways you could better utilize your funds (paying bills, saving for retirement, family vacation fund, setting up a fund for your children). If after three days you have weighed your options and you're still convinced that you have the funds to purchase the item, return to the store and buy it. If the item is not there, you can always check with other locations. Or forget it. Maybe it wasn't meant to be.

The bottom line is to train yourselves to reconsider any purchases that are not absolute necessities. To have a solid understanding of what you "need" versus what you "want," you must distinguish between "must haves" and "would really like to haves."

The "Credit Card Discount" Strategy. Many clothing stores offer credit cards with discount incentives for using the card. They will offer you 5–10 percent discounts knowing that consumers with store credit cards will spend, on average, 35 percent more than they would without that credit card. The credit card creates access to capital. If you are carrying $50 in your pocket without any line of credit you will only spend $50 within any given store. However, if you have a $200 line of credit within a store then statistics show that you will spend 35 percent more because you know you can make additional purchases. If you purchases $200 worth of clothes and get a 10 percent discount you will have spent $180 (10 percent of $200 equals a $20 discount). So if you had carried only cash, and limited your purchases to $50, you'd have saved an additional $130 even with the discount.

The "Lure" Sales Strategy. Stores have done research showing that certain scents and music lure Black males into stores. There is a reason they are playing your favorite songs as you walk by the store. They are finding ways to reach into your pocket!

Final thoughts: Never shop when you are:

- *Excited or bored,* as these feelings fuel frivolous purchases.
- *Sad,* because this emotion can trigger guilt purchases and lead to shopping addictions. Whenever you feel down you'll want to shop.
- *Hungry,* because you will purchase food you do not need but that looked good to you at the time in the store.

The question that you should be asking if you have not asked it already is, "What am I spending my money on if it is not consumption?" The opposite of consumption (putting your money into assets that lose value) is investment (putting your money into assets that go up in value). Four of the most common vehicles that you can invest your money into are stocks, bonds, real estate, and entrepreneurship. Let's discuss each of them.

1. *Stocks*
   a. The outstanding capital of a company or corporation
   b. The shares of a particular company or corporation
   c. The certificate of ownership of such stock: stock certificate

Simply put, stock is a way of dividing up ownership of a company. You can go to Starbucks and purchase coffee to be a customer. Or you can purchase *stock* in Starbucks and become part owner of the company. As an owner, you have a stake in every cup of coffee that is sold. The more shares you purchase, the larger your stake becomes. But as the market moves, stocks can increase or decrease in value.

2. *Bonds*
    a. A certificate of ownership of a specified debt due to be paid by a government or corporation to an individual holder and usually bearing a fixed rate of interest.

Both governments and corporations need capital to operate. Employers have to pay for salaries, supplies, and facilities. Governments have to pay for education, welfare, Social Security, Medicaid, and the Iraq War. One of the ways to pay for these expenses is to borrow from individuals by issuing bonds. When you purchase a bond from a company or government you are essentially lending that entity money on the condition that you get back your original investment *plus* interest.

3. *Real Estate*
    a. Land plus anything permanently fixed to it, including buildings, sheds, and other items attached to the structure.

Whether you're buying your first home or a piece of investment property on the side, owning real estate has always been part of the American dream and one of the best ways of accumulating wealth.

4. *Entrepreneurship*
    a. The organization, management, and assumption of risks involved in running a business or enterprise.
    b. Taking a chance for a new opportunity.

Owning and operating your own business has proven to bring the highest return of all investment vehicles. However, this investment also brings the greatest risk. But it's a risk worth taking when you are investing in your own ideas. Then there are those who prefer to invest in other people's ideas. These investors are called venture capitalists.

Before you begin investing your money in anything, there are a few things that you must do to prepare yourself.

Prepare a Budget. We must pay closer attention to our spending habits. There's an old saying that you can tell someone's values by looking at their checkbook register. I cannot tell you how many friends who, after being put on a budget for the first time, have said things like:

- "I would have never thought I spent that much money at the bar in a month."
- "I need to stop eating out so much!"
- "My girl is just going to have to learn to be happy with pizza!"
- "I didn't know that my closet full of sneakers cost that much!"

A realistic budget is the most important piece of the financial plan. It can be time-consuming when you first begin to organize your finances. However, as with any other financial habit, if we make a diligent effort to incorporate the language and actions of economic empowerment into our daily lives, we will be richly rewarded. Sixty percent of America is spending more money than they earn every month because they have not learned the habit of budgeting.

Eliminate Credit Card Debt. Many people feel that it's not important to eliminate credit card debt before investing in the market. Many credit cards have variable interest rates as high as 30 percent. The national average annual percentage rate is approximately 15 percent. As of this writing, the average credit card balance in each U.S. household is around $9,000 and steadily increasing. If you have $5,000 in cash, and have a credit card balance of $9,000, it does not make sense to put that $5,000 at risk to *hopefully* get a good return in the stock market when you are *certain* that you have to pay 15 percent on your credit cards. Whatever extra cash you have should go to pay down your credit card debt.

Prepare An Emergency Fund. It is vital to have three to six months of living expenses saved up before you invest in the market. When Detroit teachers were on strike for eight days in 2006, many teachers at the credit union were applying for loans because they didn't have enough savings to last for more than a week. These savings should be placed in a high-yield savings account that pays a good interest rate on the money. A regular checking account may have a 0 percent rate, which means you are actually losing money to inflation.

Inflation is the gradual loss of any currency's value. When the general level of prices rise in relation to the amount of money in circulation, that's inflation. Inflation is why you could buy a candy bar in the '70s for a nickel but now pay as much as a dollar for the same candy bar. Inflation is a major reason why gas prices continue to increase, making it more expensive to drive and transport goods to stores. If you are keeping your money under the mattress, in a safe in the basement, or anywhere that it's not earning interest, then your money is losing value to inflation as you read this. Putting your money into a high-yield savings account like ING Direct, Emigrant Direct, and One United Bank will earn you enough interest to outpace inflation and grow in real value. I saved the best for last: One United Bank is a Black-owned bank that gives one of the highest rates of return in the country as of this writing.

PAID IN FULL

One day while watching CNN, I saw an older gentleman being interviewed who was worth over $2 million even though he had never in his life earned more than $11 an hour. How did he do it? He simply made a practice of investing his money and living within his means. When he paid his monthly bills, he made sure to pay himself by making monthly deposits in his investment account. Investing is not just for the rich, but for all income and age levels. But the less you earn, the more important it is to watch your expenditures. Make sure you keep a cushion for any financial setbacks (job loss, salary cuts, rising prices, or medical emergencies). Regardless of your income or financial position, it's up to you to begin saving toward financial independence today!

BLACK MALES AND CREDIT

Every successful financial plan relies on having clean credit. If we are to achieve the goal of increased home and business ownership in the African American community, good credit is the first step toward accomplishing it. I have seen too many opportunities missed because we have not taken the time to "clean up" our credit.

Knowing how to boost your FICO score is one of the most important factors in improving your credit. A FICO score is a three-digit number that determines the interest you will pay on your credit cards, home mortgage, and even whether you will be approved for a new purchase. FICO, the Fair Isaac Corporation, single-handedly created this three-digit score that controls your livelihood in many ways.

There are five elements of the FICO score. They are listed below along with their weight of importance.

1. Record of making timely bill payments: 35 percent
2. Total balance on your credit cards and other loans compared to your total credit limit: 30 percent
3. Length of credit history: 15 percent
4. New accounts, recent loan applications, and credit inquiries: 10 percent
5. Mixture of credit cards and loans: 10 percent

Now that you know these are the key factors, how can you raise your FICO score?

Pay your bills on time. There is no excuse for late payments. As soon as I receive a bill, I pay it. It was a very difficult habit to establish, because instinct says to throw the bill on the dresser, preferably under a pile of other envelopes, and avoid it like the plague. Another bill-paying strategy is to designate one day each month where you do nothing but pay bills. No matter what you are doing, stop and pay your bills. The only downfall to this is that all bills are not due at the same time, opening the door for procrastination. If the fixed monthly cycle is your preferred strategy, designating two days a month might be more appropriate.

Better still is just to pay the bills as they come. One missed payment can lower your FICO score by 50 to 100 points. If you miss a whole month of payments, a 700 FICO score can easily drop to 526. I understand that it may be tempting to act as if bills that you cannot afford do not exist, but such negative habits are severely hindering the economic growth of our community. I challenge you to be responsible about each bill that comes into your home. We have all had times when we fell behind or missed a payment—myself included. But the key is how we recover from these mistakes to diligently create a positive credit history. Responsibility and accountability are key principles of the economic empowerment movement.

The debt-to-credit-limit ratio. Your debt-to-credit-limit (D/C) ratio is an important issue as well. Let's say you have a $3,000 balance on a credit card and a credit limit of $6,000. Your D/C would be 50 percent ($3,000/$6,000). This is an important number that accounts for a large part (30 percent) of your FICO score. Continuing with the above example, if you pay off a $1,000 balance on one of your cards with a credit limit of $2,500, I would advise you *not* to cancel that card. Your credit limit would decrease from $6,000 to $3,500 (remember you had a $2,500 limit on the card). Since you just paid $1,000 of your total balance owed, your new balance owed decreased from $3,000 to $2,000. Your new D/C ratio would now be 57 percent ($2,000/$3,500), higher than the previous number of 50 percent. So the end result of your responsible behavior—paying bills and reducing debt—would be an increase in your debt-to-credit-limit ratio and a drop in your FICO score. The better move when paying off a credit card is to cut up your card and leave the account open—unless there is an annual fee. (There's no sense in wasting $50 to $70 a year on a card you will never use.)

Your credit history. The length of your credit history is very important as well. If you must cancel a card, make sure you cancel the newest ones first. The longer your credit lines have been open, the more data Fair Isaac Corporation has to determine your FICO score. Protect your cards with the longest history. If you must cancel a card, cancel one card, then wait a month. Then check and see if your score was negatively affected. If not, do the same for each additional card you want to cancel.

Beware of new accounts. You want to be careful not to apply for too many cards at once. This sends a red flag to lenders. Steer clear of having too many retailer cards. When you're at the sales counter, it can be very tempting to allow the checkout clerk to coerce you into a store savings card that will supposedly open the door to "extreme savings." Just keep in mind that (according to *The Millionaire Next Door*) the top five credit cards of millionaires (and the percent of millionaires who own them) are as follows:

1. Visa (59 percent)
2. MasterCard (56 percent)
3. Sears (43 percent)
4. JC Penney (30.4 percent)
5. American Express Gold (28.6 percent)

The truly wealthy avoid retail credit card traps. They use the cards they need responsibly and with caution so as not to accumulate unnecessary, overpriced debt.

Lenders like to see a good mix of installment loans (e.g., monthly car notes, monthly mortgage notes) along with your credit cards. Installment loans show just how reliable one can be, especially if payments have been made for an extended period of time, as well as in a timely fashion.

USING CREDIT CARDS WISELY

As consumption rises in the Black community, so does consumer debt. The incorrect assumption is often made that getting a credit card is simply a matter of opening an account. This misconception has led to many financial disasters. As African Americans, and specifically as Black males, it is critical that you understand the most important factors to consider when selecting a credit card:

1. Make sure that there are *no* hidden fees for having and using the card.
2. Check the interest rate. If you have a decent credit history, you should be able to get an introductory rate below 5 percent. This rate typically lasts for six months to a year. You might be able to get a 0 percent rate for this period. The FICO score (credit score) is a key number in this situation. If your score is above 720, you should be able to get an excellent rate. If it is below 720, you might do better to focus on raising your score above 720 before you apply for a card. With a higher score, you can demand lower rates.
3. Know your grace period. This is the time between the statement date and the date when your payment is due. If you pay your bill in full during this period, you should owe no interest. But this grace period doesn't work if you carry a balance. The moment you carry a balance over until the next month, you begin to pay interest. You might want

to shop around for the longest grace period. The standard grace period is twenty-five days. Other cards offer a twenty-day grace period while some give consumers no grace period at all (steer clear of these). Read each statement carefully, as many companies will switch grace periods and hide this information in the small print. It's a good idea to check your due date each month to see if the grace period has been shortened.

4. What is the billing cycle? Is it the average daily balance (good) or the two-cycle average daily balance (not so good)? Let's say last month you charged $5,000 and paid off $4,800, leaving a $200 balance. With an average daily balance billing cycle, you will be charged interest only on the $200 that you didn't pay off. With two-cycle billing, you owe interest on the full $5,000 because this card looks at a balance for the previous two months.

5. How do they calculate the minimum due? Most cards charge 1.5 to 2.5 percent of the outstanding balance. The lower this number, the lower the amount you have to pay back each month. But the less you pay off, the more interest builds up. I strongly urge that you pay off more than the minimum due—the entire balance, if possible.

6. Pay on time!

7. Look out for mistakes. Sometimes credit cards double-charge you by mistake.

More than the credit card itself, the most important thing is how you use the card. Do *not* use these cards for everyday purposes. Store your card in a safe place in your home, where you will not be tempted to use it frequently. The purpose of this credit card should be twofold:

1. To establish a credit history.
2. To give you extra protection in case of an emergency.

In the first place, you should never spend money that you cannot pay back immediately. If you want to purchase a book, and want to use your card to establish a credit history, don't buy the book if you don't have the funds to immediately pay off the bill. When I use my credit card, I charge whatever item I purchase and on the following day I pay the entire balance on my credit card. If you cannot do that, then you must do without the item (unless it is a serious *need* such as food, water, lodging, or essential clothing).

Make sure you get a sufficient line of credit. Ideally, the card should be able to cover at least three months of expenses during an emergency. Using the card in an emergency should not replace your goal of building an emergency fund—remember you need to save at least six months of living expenses. Use the card as a backup when your emergency funds run out.

At the end of the day, credit card companies are in business to make a profit. And judging by the fact that over 60 percent of Americans spend more money than they make, the credit cards are doing an excellent job maximizing their profits. Simply put, the more you pay, the more money they make. These companies work within a legal system to make it difficult for you to navigate through all the red tape. They send long contracts with tricky wording in fine print and letters they know you won't read, plus they change the billing cycle. The more irresponsible and uninformed we are, the more money they make.

HOME OWNERSHIP

Buying your own home is no small venture, and it's one that requires considerable thought and planning. Anyone who has purchased a house will agree that the process is time-consuming, tedious, and costly. But people still do it because it's one of the most important investments a person can make. When deciding what kind of home you purchase, you have a complex decision to make. The total cost of your home, as well as the interest rate and the payments you are required to make, will have a huge effect on your future financial state.

In their book *The Millionaire Next Door*, Thomas J. Stanley and William D. Danko argue that you should "never purchase a home that requires a mortgage that is more than twice your household's total annual realized income." While this statement may be an oversimplification, the principle behind it is a sound one.

When purchasing a home, remember to "act your own wage." Choose a home priced within the limits of what you can afford to pay. I have witnessed many people looking for a new home without any idea of how much they can actually afford. How do you think the whole mortgage crisis got started in the first place? I urge everyone to do your math *before* hunting for your new home.

The subprime credit market crash that began in 2006 was possible because so many people failed to prepare themselves properly, thus making them more susceptible to predatory lending practices. Don't let a mortgage broker do the math for you, as he or she will push for the highest loan so they can make the highest commission. Brokers will try to find a way to stretch you beyond your means, making themselves a nice commission while you lose your sanity trying to overextend your budget to afford your mortgage payments.

This is the essence of predatory lending. Remember that everyone who has ever filed for bankruptcy or foreclosure was initially approved for a loan from the bank. Know what you can and cannot afford before you meet with a mortgage broker. Buying a home should not be your only goal, rather you should be buying a home that you can comfortably maintain while living in it. "The rich rule over the poor, and the borrower is servant to the lender." (Proverbs 22:7).

One good strategy is to purchase an "imaginary house." Calculate the amount of money you think you will be able to afford and then open a savings account. With your "house fund," put a down payment into your new account that will come as close to 20 percent as you can afford. Each month after you make the down payment put the calculated mortgage payment for your new imaginary home in the account. Without fail, make mortgage payments into your savings account every month until you have the 20 percent down payment that you will need for your imaginary home. If you find that you are able to make these payments while still living comfortably, then you are on your way to having that new house.

Many people have discussed the possibilities of paying off your mortgage early. I have always been a huge fan of early mortgage payments. However, you shouldn't start paying down your mortgage until you have established an adequate emergency fund in case of unexpected circumstances. There are a number of pros and cons relative to paying off a mortgage early. Once you have purchased your home and made a decision to investigate an early pay-off, ask a financial advisor to evaluate your personal circumstances.

We need more Black males to realize the dream of owning their own home. To come home to something that we own is truly a magical feeling. But we also need to be diligent enough not to leave our financial futures in the hands of others. Make sure to do your own research and personally cross every *t* and dot every *i* Don't be afraid to invest in a competent financial advisor to assist you with this tedious process. Always be willing to invest in professionals whose intellectual capital will enhance your quality of life.

With predatory lending being such a hot topic, let's end this section by reviewing three simple steps on how to avoid it.

Step One: Improve Your FICO Score

If you are thinking of purchasing a home, the right time to start thinking about improving your credit score is now. You should give yourself a year to improve your FICO score by doing the following:

- **First:** Check Your Credit Report
    - Seventy-five percent of all reports have errors on them. You are allowed to obtain one free report per year from each of the credit agencies (Equifax, Experian, Transunion). Go to www.annualcreditreport. com, download your reports, and get rid of any small balances you might have forgotten about.

- **Second:** Pay Your Bills on Time
  - Use your bank's auto-payment service to assure that the money is automatically deducted from your account. Make sure you have an accurate budget and leave enough funds in your account to cover bill payments.

- **Third:** Pay Down Debts
  - Eliminate all balances on your credit cards as soon as possible. Avoid being seduced by credit card companies with special offers. You will never hear of someone becoming a millionaire because their credit card company offered them frequent-flier miles.

- **Fourth:** Do Not Cancel Old Accounts
  - Thirty percent of your FICO score is your balance/lending ratio. If you already have an account open, canceling that account can lower your FICO score.

- **Fifth:** Don't Fear Credit Counselors
  - Going to a credit counselor or a debt consolidation agency is not viewed negatively by FICO.

- **Sixth:** Steer Clear of Bankruptcy
  - Bankruptcy is even harder to file for as a result of new legislation passed by President George W. Bush. You can have up to

200 points deducted from your credit score and this will stay on your report for ten years.

- **Seventh:** Be Patient!
  - Nothing happens overnight. This process will take time.

If you follow these steps and your FICO score stays below 650, then do not purchase a home. Give yourself enough time to raise your score. There's nothing wrong with waiting and there's no such thing in the housing market as a deal that's here today but won't return in some form tomorrow.

Step Two: Know Your Limits

As stated before, a household budget is crucial to home ownership. Do not allow the bank to decide how much you can afford. If you Google the phrase "mortgage calculator" you will be able to find many websites that will assist you in this process. And beware of tricky gimmicks like "interest-only" mortgages. Many Americans were duped by these mortgages, which seem less expensive because the borrower is only required to pay the interest on the loan. But many uneducated borrowers did not realize that this introductory period would soon expire, leading to an increase of up to 500 percent. A few hours of research could have avoided the millions of foreclosures that we are currently seeing across this nation.

Step Three: Get Three Opinions

- **First:** Consult with a mortgage professional. Find a trustworthy mortgage lender you are comfortable working with. Nothing beats a professional opinion in these matters.
- **Second:** Seek an unbiased party. Ask someone who does not have a conflicting interest. While it's good to hear from a qualified mortgage lender, such professionals may be interested in earning a commission. The larger the loan you take out, the larger their commission. Predatory lending practices have caused many people to take out loans on homes that they cannot afford.
- **Third:** Research for *yourself*. The time of going to the financial professional without researching the various products for oneself is over. If I steal a car, and I know that I will be arrested if I get caught, does that mean that I don't need a lawyer? Well, no. But having a basic knowledge of the law can help keep me out of trouble. The same applies to our finances.

To educate yourself and find helpful advice for home buyers, go to the following websites:

Federal Housing Administration: www.fha.com
U.S. Department of Housing and Urban Development: www.hud.gov

INVESTING IN YOUR COMMUNITY

During the years when I was an equity trader on Wall Street, and more recently, as a financial planner, I have fielded many questions. One of the most common questions I have been asked is "What is the best area to invest in in this market?"

The answer depends on whom you ask. Many brokers claim that stocks are poised for a strong rally. Others say that bonds are more attractive. I have often heard that real estate is the best way to accumulate wealth for the long run. But there is another area of investment that is not talked about as frequently. This area of investment has *tremendous* potential for an almost unlimited upside. *What is it?* you ask.

I'll give you a clue: you wake up in it every day and go to sleep in it every night. You take your children to school in it, attend block parties in it, and your family and friends may also live here. If you haven't guessed by now, I'm referring to your own community. An investment in your community might just be the greatest investment you can make. But how does one invest in a community? And what are the returns?

Before I answer, let me jump back in time for a moment. After graduating from the University of Michigan Business School in 1999, I spent the next five years working on Wall Street as an equity trader—four of those years at the largest NASDAQ trading firm in the country. Out of nearly three hundred traders on the floor, I noticed that there were only three to five Black traders at any given time. This fact did not make me uncomfortable, because my primary objective was not to create social change, but to make money. And that's exactly what I did.

But during my final year on Wall Street my aunt called me to ask, "What is a stock?" Despite my being involved in the world of finance for many years, I realized that many members of my own family did not know the important information I took for granted. Once I recognized this lack of knowledge within the Black community, I decided to pursue a new career. I wanted to educate my people about the importance of financial literacy. The best way for me to do this was to pursue a career in financial planning.

When I turned in my letter of resignation to the equity trading firm and began to prepare for my new job as a financial planner, I was excited, to say the least. I had visions of educating *all* members of my community and communicated these visions to my new employer. Then I was hit with a harsh reality: "I understand that you want to educate your community," a supervisor told me. "However, unless you are working with high net worth individuals you are wasting your time."

This crushed my spirit. If my own mother walked into my office I could not work with her because according to that firm, she was too poor to be worth my time. I told my supervisor I needed a few more days to contemplate the offer and then I simply walked out. And then on Tuesday, September 14, 2004, Optimum Capital Management became a reality.

For the next twelve months I did not earn a single dollar. I spent that time researching all the firms that had given me offers, reading two to three books per month, working with Crown Financial Ministries to learn biblical principles of managing finances, conducting free seminars throughout my community, and creating a personal financial literacy course for colleges (and one for the U.S. Department of Justice). I started a campaign to teach financial literacy to individuals of all income levels—whether rich or poor, Black or White, male or female, young or old. My target audience included all parts of our community, from university students to members of unions, churches, even gangs. All were welcome, whether residents of inner-city neighborhoods or public housing. I have traveled across the United States and have even gone as far as South Africa to teach this vital information to *all* those who need it.

I am not trying to brag or boast about my company. Many of us have skills and abilities that we can contribute to the advancement of our communities. If you are one of those who are too apathetic to contribute, then I suggest that you put this essay down and give it to someone who is willing to assist in the movement. If you are one who wants to assist in the growth of the community, then I have listed below a few ways and places where you can contribute.

Community Businesses

There are many businesses in your community—restaurants, bakeries, schools, and libraries—and all are a reflection of the character of the community. Outsiders get a sense of the community by the upkeep, quality of service, and ambiance within these local institutions. Frequent investment is crucial to property value and quality of living. An increased flow of time and money through the community will be reflected in property values and ultimately in improved quality of life for the community's residents. So make sure you eat in your community restaurants, donate books to your local libraries and schools, and frequent the stores and shops in your community.

Entrepreneurship

According to *Black Economics: Solutions for Economic and Community Empowerment*, by Jawanza Kunjufu, the number of business owners per thousand people breaks down as follows: "107 Lebanese, 93 Syrians, 89 Koreans, 65 Japanese, 64 White, 60 Chinese, 30 Columbians, 21 Jamaicans, 17 Hispanics, and 9 for African Americans." Why are we so afraid to step out of our comfort zone and become entrepreneurs in our communities?

How much return did Bob Johnson, Russell Simmons, or Oprah Winfrey get on their original investment in their own company? The number is too large for any ordinary calculator to count. Successful entrepreneurship provides one of the largest returns on your investment. So I challenge you to open your own business in you own community. Below are the four steps to follow before you get started.

Step One: Find Your Passion

Our creator gave all of us skills at birth. No matter how humble you are, there must be something you can do better than anybody else. What is it that you're always thinking and talking about? What skills and talents do you have that can translate into dollars? One strategy you might want to consider is volunteering. Not only does it help the community, it gives you a chance to try out new things. After all, if you're willing to do something for free then it just might be your passion. That passion will give you the strength to do the extra work that's needed to create a successful company. Within your passion you will find the excitement that will always grab your attention and help you to focus when all around you seems to be in chaos. Talk to any millionaire, and more often than not they'll say that they've found their passion in life. What is yours?

Step Two: Have a Vision

"Where there is no vision, the people perish . . ."
—Proverbs 29:18

If you are driving a car, but do not know your final destination, how are you supposed to know if you're off course? Within the word *destination* you'll find the root of the word *destiny*. Do you know what your destiny holds? I challenge you today to take authority and control of your life. I challenge you to have a vision of your destiny. Where will you be in ten years? Twenty years? Thirty?

Maybe you don't have a vision for today—that's not the end of the world. But make no mistake, we need soldiers with focus and clear intentions in this economic empowerment movement, soldiers who can lead our communities to a higher level of economic development. Without vision you will lead your community nowhere but to a state of chaos and confusion. We already have enough of that in the Black community, and I for one am tired of it. Lead or get out of the way!

Step Three: Collect the Necessary Resources for Success

Now that you have a vision, you must collect the necessary resources to bring that vision to fruition. And the most important of all resources is knowledge, no matter where you are in your educational development.

High school dropouts: We need you to get your GED to participate in this movement. If you aren't willing to go to college—which isn't for everyone—then you need to find the resources necessary to develop a skilled trade so that you can help build our communities.

High school students: For brothers who have visions of higher education, talk to your school counselors to help you research the best school for you. Make sure to research all the scholarships that are available to you on websites like FastWeb.com, Scholarship America.org, or scholarships.com. After you've written at *least* twenty essays (yes, I said twenty) to apply for at least twenty scholarships, apply for as much financial aid as possible.

Do not limit your search to local institutions. They're cost-effective, and I know many students who have attained success with degrees from these institutions. But why should you assume that Harvard, Brown, Yale, and Princeton are not options for you? If you've got the grades, it *is* possible to attend an Ivy League school. And don't leave historically black colleges and universities (HBCUs) out of the equation either. The education and networking opportunities you'll receive at a Howard, Hampton, or Morehouse are tremendous. Whether you choose an Ivy League or an HBCU, it takes both vision and desire to see beyond the boundaries of your immediate community.

I am from Detroit, but my world did not start and end there. I attended the University of Michigan, where I graduated from the top-ranked business program in the country. Then I had the vision to leave Michigan to pursue something larger than my surroundings. I urge you to do the same. But *never* forget where you came from. Use the knowledge that you acquire in higher education and in life to return home and help to build up your community.

College students: Do not be limited to your required curriculum. Now is the time to grab every opportunity to explore new ways to develop yourself and your community. The more you work outside of school, the more experience you can add to your résumé and the more attractive you will be to employers. Talk to as many business owners as possible, mentor high school students who want to go to school. Try to take a semester abroad. There's no better way to learn that the world is bigger than your community.

College graduates: Brothers, we need you to continue to develop your mind. When I was starting my company, Amazon.com became my best friend, and still is. If you are the smartest person in your group, you're in the wrong group. Always push yourself to find people who will stretch and challenge you mentally. We need soldiers who are willing and able to contribute to an intellectual think tank that can move the community forward as a whole, economically, spiritually, mentally, physically, and socially.

It's often said that you can tell a lot about someone by the company they keep. Brothers, I know you are loyal to your friends, and loyalty is important. But in the quest for intellectual and spiritual development, you will find that some friends are no longer on the same level as you. I am not saying to cut them off, but I am saying to recognize the path you are on. If they are not willing to join you, they may drag you down with their acceptance of mediocrity. We have spent too many years in shackles to allow our own people to entrap our progress. We must break free from *all* bondage.

I challenge you to meet as many positive people as possible until you meet that one person who catapults you to the next level through their contribution to your life. Feel free to consider me as a resource as well. Don't think that I am any better than you are because I am writing this essay. If you want to reach out to me please do so. I am accessible.

Capital is another important resource that you must acquire. I would not have been able to start Optimum Capital Management unless I had saved the funds I needed to resign from my job. But looking back, I saw many ways I could have saved more resources. That year I went without earning a dollar meant many dinners of Cheese Nips, tuna fish, and sunflower seeds—or nothing at all. I lasted twelve months on savings alone, but had I been more diligent I could have been more comfortable during that time. Nonetheless, it was a small price to pay for me to be able to uplift communities across the country.

Step Four: Write a Five-Step Plan of Action

Knowledge alone is not power. I know many smart people who are penniless. Knowledge plus *action* equals power. I challenge you to write out a five-step plan of action today. This plan of action should only include steps of substance. Not just "working hard," but tangible steps of action like the following:

- Call the local community center to sign up for a GED course.
- Call that brother with his own business to learn how he got started.
- Fill out a college application and send it in.
- Research scholarships to fill out applications and send them in.
- Create a budget so that you can monitor your personal spending habits.
- Buy some life insurance and have a will written so that if something happens to you your family won't suffer.

- Learn how to write out an elaborate business plan.
- Log onto www.inc-it-now.com to fill out the form necessary to start the company that you have been researching.
- Have regular conversations with your lady friend or partner (if you are a gay Black male) to ensure that you're on the same page, because you know that settling down with a soulmate is the "alpha and omega" of your success.

Take some time to write out this plan of action. The odds of achieving your goals increase tremendously when you write them down. Your plan will grow and change as you grow and change as a person. This is fine, as long as you keep your eyes on the prize. It won't happen right away, but remain on course. If you find your passion, develop a vision, acquire the necessary resources, and write out a plan of action. Then it might take six months, a year, three, or even five years—but you *will* be successful.

Investing in Our Youth

The youth of our communities are crying out for our assistance and support. Investing in the youth of our communities yields the kind of returns that are the most immediate and most fulfilling. My firm started a youth financial literacy organization called All About Business (AAB). I have been volunteering my time at least four days a month for over six years teaching financial literacy within the local school system.

Meeting once per week with these students, I saw them grasp the information so well that they were ready to become teachers themselves. It was amazing to see a fifteen-year-old schooling a group of adults about complex financial principles. Not only did these youths conduct their own seminars, they began to embody the principles they were learning. Many researched and received scholarships to school. Due to their newfound networking abilities, many received internships. Emphasis on the principles of entrepreneurship has led to the formation of many different businesses, from an event planning company to a car service, a construction company, a business-themed board game, and a clothing line, to name a few. As I am writing this, ten of my students are writing what will be the first book written by teenagers to educate adults about financial literacy. We must raise the level of expectations for our youth in every way, and All About Business is an example of the kind of changes these increased expectations can create.

Bringing a smile to a youngster's face is one of the most personally rewarding experiences there is. I will always spend time with the youth in my community because I continue to see so many positive results. How many young Bob Johnsons, Warren Buffetts, or Bill Clintons will never reach their full potential because we didn't take the time to invest in them? I urge everyone reading this to volunteer at your local school and talk to the children. Career days, tutor programs, and after-school programs are all opportunities to spend time with children of your community. The children are, of course, our future, and investing in their lives is also an investment in yours.

The Bible says, "But if any provide not for his own, and specially for those of his own house, he hath denied the faith, and is worse than an infidel." (1 Timothy 5:8).

I urge you to think about how you are contributing to your own communities. If you are not active, then how can you get active? Many people look to politicians to create change, but fail to realize that they can create positive change in their own communities. Participate in your community, give (time and money) to your community, and most of all *respect* your community.

NEXT STEPS

I know that for some of you, many of these concepts and principles are complex and perhaps difficult to understand. However, to make this essay any more simplistic would have been an insult to the intelligence level that runs in our race. We are the race that created math and science. There is no reason why financial illiteracy should plague our communities. When I first learned about tax-deferred accounts I was perplexed as well but that was not my cue to give up. Instead I picked up another book, read another article, and asked somebody else to help me understand the concept.

I know many people who have read books about financial literacy but have yet to progress because they are stuck in the information-gathering stage. How many plans in the Black community are going to live and die on the drawing board because we lack the faith and fortitude to take action and implement them? Remember, knowledge is not enough! I urge you to take action today. Reach into your pocket to pay a qualified financial advisor whom you can trust. So many of us will knock the door down to purchase a PlayStation for our children but hesitate to pay a professional who can actually enhance our lives. Gather friends and family to form financial literacy support groups. This is a new language for many of you, and I don't expect anyone to learn it overnight. But we must do all that is necessary to make sure we're walking the path toward economic empowerment and financial independence.

My grandmother used to tell a story about a horse who rides

into a dark tunnel. When the horse refuses to continue into the blackness, his master takes out a handkerchief, blindfolds the horse, and they ride on until the master sees a huge hole in the road ahead. Traveling at such a fast speed, the master knew it was impossible to stop the horse. Thinking quickly, the master jumped to safety just in time. Meanwhile the horse fell to his death at the bottom of the hole. Whose fault was it that the horse died? The horse's fault!

Without basic financial literacy, without the essential knowledge of how to control our finances, without the ability to think for ourselves, we are no better off than that horse being led into a dark tunnel blindfolded. As long as we rely upon "the master" to rule our destinies, we are no better than the slaves on the plantation who had no say in their financial destinies. I'm not a slave, are you? Of course not. So don't act like it!

5

Taking Care of Your
Physical Health

By Kendrick B. Nathaniel

I begin this impartation humbly, by asking that all who read this, my gift to you, receive it in the same loving spirit with which I deliver it. May this essay serve as a meaningful source of knowledge and empowerment to help you seize control of your physical well-being. You may already know that Black males generally are in worse health than any other racial group in America. We have twice the rate of cancer and heart disease compared with White males, five times the rate of AIDS infection, and our young men are the number-one victims of violence. The reasons why are numerous: lack of affordable health care, subpar health education, stress, violence, toxic environments, and negative lifestyle choices such as lack of proper nutrition, overeating, smoking, drinking, drugs, unsafe sex, and failure to exercise. My focus in this essay is how to reverse those trends. And I believe it starts with loving yourselves enough to take care of yourselves. We are all of one source, no matter what source you may claim.

So before we begin, let me give you some information about me, so that you can find some parts of yourself in myself. I drew my first breath on March 11, 1968, at 10:35 AM, in New York's Columbia Presbyterian, the same hospital where Malcolm X drew his last breath, three years prior. I grew up in the Bronx, in the Throggs Neck projects, on Sampson Avenue to be exact. Throggs Neck was so out there in the Bronx that the subway didn't even reach that far. Nevertheless, we were the place to be. All the locks on all our lampposts had been broken. For all you " '80s babies," let me fill you in—that's where the power for the turntables and speakers came from. And if you don't know, now you know. Kool Herc, Grandmaster Flash, and damn near every other New York DJ you can name used to come through TNP and tear it up. The MC might have had something to say, but he couldn't even get on until the DJ got it hot.

As hot as those parties were, they weren't hot enough to keep me from the lure of hanging out with my friends and getting into trouble. Maybe if I would have spent more time listening to the DJ, I could have avoided the constant flow of problems that always found their way to me, all the time!

My dad left when I was four years old, back when we were living on Eagle Avenue, near the Grand Concourse. I'll never forget that day—him taking my older brother and me to the movies, then out to ride our bikes. I vividly remember watching him walking away from us on the Grand Concourse. I guess I was too young to even fathom that I wouldn't hear from him again until I was twenty-eight years old. Fortunately, he left me in the hands of a super woman, if not the Superwoman—my mom. And so I became yet another product of a single mother's home, for better and for worse.

When I tell you that I was a bad child, it's a gross understatement. I went to P.S. 72, but not for an education. I went there to fight, and that's what I did—every single day! I fought so much that all the other kids constantly followed me home to see the show. And now I realize, that that's all it was: me putting on a show to get attention. This was my way of masking all the fears, the fear of not fitting in, of someone realizing that my kicks didn't come from Modell's, but from the big bin in the middle of a Grand Union supermarket aisle. I would suppress these fears for the better part of my life until well into my late twenties. Now I realize that my mom managed her income, public assistance and all, so that we ate regularly and well at home, as opposed to the junk food that was readily available on every other corner in the hood.

As a matter of fact, I was so bad, Mom packed up our entire family—with me kicking and screaming—and moved us down to Walterboro, South Carolina, where she was born and raised. Before we left New York, I got myself expelled from two public grade schools and one parochial school. Yet I wanted to stay so bad that I jumped out of the U-Haul truck when we stopped to say goodbye to my aunt in Harlem. I would not learn how big a sacrifice my mom was making until many years later, when I realized that she'd left a really good job, at Alexander's Warehouse in Hunts Point, only to be reduced to a series of menial and degrading jobs in South Carolina. She did everything from being a seasonal housekeeper, to raking leaves in White families' yards, to working in a veneer plant alongside my grandfather, making floors from wood chips twelve hours a day. And I had no idea she was doing all this just to save my life.

How could I have had any idea? I was too busy fighting, even in South Carolina. The only difference was that in New York I chose to fight, but when I got to South Carolina I had no choice!

I'm sure a lot of you can relate—put a hardhead from da BX in a small town in South Carolina, with all the freshest wears—you know, 69ers, two-tone Lee's, Kangaroos, Kangols, Gazelles, BVD nylon tees and tanks. And I wasn't bad-looking, either! Now you got problems. Or at least I had problems.

As much as I tried to do the right thing, those Walterboro dudes were not having it. They would tell me they wanted to fight me just because I was from New York. As a result, I would have to fight just about every day, sometimes a couple of times a day, because down there, if you beat up a kid with a brother, you usually had to beat up his brother, too. Now I had an older brother, three years my senior, but somehow all the madness seemed to escape him—probably because he was really into the basketball thing. I've never really been much of an athlete my-self. I tried football once, in New York. This kid hit me too hard, and it was on and poppin'! Needless to say, that was my last day on the team. Although I never played sports, I've always had a very physical lifestyle, eventually working as a personal trainer, a bodyguard, and even as a model. The key for me was finding a way to transform that negative energy (fighting) into something more constructive. Once your energy is right, everything else just falls into line. But it took a while for me to reach the turning point.

I spent several more years fighting until my brother left home for the navy, and my mom met a man who would later become her husband. At this point I realized that coexisting with a "father figure"—after not having to do so for my entire life—was not go-ing to happen. More to the point, I wasn't going to make it in my mom's house too much longer. My brother kept calling home talking about how great navy life was, and that was all I needed to hear.

I had just one problem: by the age of seventeen I had only

"fought" my way through to the tenth grade, so a family friend suggested that I try Job Corps, and I did. That's when I first realized that I wasn't dumb—I just liked to fight more than I liked the idea of going to school. Once I made up my mind to succeed, I finished what was supposed to be an 18- to 36-month Job Corps program in just three months. I walked out of there with my GED and a brick mason's apprenticeship certificate, but that was actually the least of my accomplishments. The most important thing I gained was a sense of accomplishment that leads to greater self-respect. I took the ASVAB (Armed Services Vocational Aptitude Battery), scored high as hell, and the recruiters came running. Needless to say, I decided to follow my brother into the navy. And that was my jump-start into physical fitness.

Not really knowing what to expect in the navy, I started exercising constantly, running up, down, and all around those country roads in Walterboro. Though I wouldn't recommend it, I must admit that all the fighting had kept me in pretty good shape. Still the exercising I was doing took me to a whole other level. I was running at least a sub-five-minute mile, and I could do more push-ups, pull-ups, and jumping jacks than my recruiter. I was jacked when I got to Orlando, Florida, for basic training. I would go on to spend ten years in the U.S. Navy. Though I traveled to some of the farthest parts of the world, I spent the majority of my time based in Little Creek, Virginia, which is between Virginia Beach and Norfolk. I attended Central Texas College and Norfolk State University, where I received a B.A. in liberal arts. To describe my whole military career would take more pages than I've been allotted here, but those experiences boil down to this: of all the things I received in the navy, the most important thing by far was self-discipline. This ability to work hard toward a goal in the future has helped me in so many different ways throughout the rest of my life that I truly don't know where I would be today without it. Developing that discipline in myself also helped me to appreciate it in others, particularly my grandfather.

I briefly alluded to my mother's father earlier in this piece, but Lord knows he warrants more recognition than that. I now realize that he played a critical role in my life—most importantly, in shaping my perception of myself. My grandfather wasn't the loudest man I ever met, but he knew how to get and keep my attention when he needed me to hear him. Although most of the time he was content with me just seeing him, seeing him be the man that he was, the father to ten children, one of whom was lost shortly after birth, the husband to his wife, and most prominent in my mind, the provider for everyone who came into his presence. Six days every week, my grandfather would come home from working twelve hours at the veneer factory and proceed to chop firewood, feed his horses, feed his cow, load his pickup truck with store-bought feed and all the "slop" he'd accumulated from various relatives' houses, then drive another ten miles to feed about thirty pigs he kept on land that, to this day, I still do not know who it belonged to. Certain times of year my grandfather would return to the house, presumably exhausted, and proceed to hitch one of his horses to a plow, and plow what seemed like one of the largest fields I've ever seen. And this wasn't one of those plows you could attach to a horse and ride; this is the one you had to walk behind and hold steady, all the while ensuring that the reins kept the horse going in the right direction. Plowing was the only task that my grandfather never allowed me to try, because he knew the harm that would come to me if I made just one mistake. This man was Superman to me. And he wasn't a really big man. He was tall, his chest was kind of concave, but he was strong! He had muscles everywhere, and it was apparent that he used them constantly, because whenever he moved, his muscles did, too. Men like my grandfather didn't have to join a gym or hire a personal trainer to stay fit. It was evident that he worked hard, because he bore the scars, all about his body, from the barbed-wire fences he drew to contain his livestock, from flying chips as his ax struck the wood, to the occasional rope burn when Tom the horse wanted to go his own way with the plow.

As many times as he took his belt to my behind—and I guess I lost count around the millionth time—he was a humble, gentle soul. My grandfather was soft-spoken, never smoked, and I can't say I ever saw him take as much as a sip from those clear white milk jugs filled with "white lightning" so potent it had long since singed the labels. Elia Grant, my grandfather, was a man, a strong Black man! And I know this, because he told me every day of his life—and yet he never uttered those words. He did better than that: he showed me. Before and after every single breath he took. And I think he knew exactly what he was doing for me, his grandson who couldn't see anything without a fist being involved. Yet those chores would be my introduction to hard work, and to the ever-present idea that being a man—a Grant man—meant something.

Now you may be saying to yourself, Isn't this essay supposed to be about physical health? Yes, it is. But as I mentioned earlier, your physical health starts inside with your mind, your spirit, and with your positive energy. Without getting those in order, no amount of workout regimens or doctor visits can make you well. Of course I've always known the aesthetic value of working out— the appeal it has to the ladies. I make no bones about the fact that this did factor into my motivation for keeping it tight. But the main reason I've been able to maintain my very physical lifestyle is that I started exercising regularly at a very young age, so it has been a part of me for over twenty-five years now. Maybe you used to exercise when you were younger but you fell off. Or maybe you're a Madden PlayStation champion who's never broken an honest sweat in your life. No matter where you find yourself, physical fitness can and will be that edge that puts you way under, way over, or somewhere in the middle. You don't have to start by running a triathlon, but you do have to be patient and consistent, and that means you have to practice self-discipline.

When I returned to New York during the Tyson Beckford era of modeling in the early 1990s, so many years after my mom rescued me from that city, I decided to pursue a career in modeling. I would soon discover that it was common practice for male models to moonlight as personal trainers. That was right up my alley, although I did it without a certification for about a year, because money wasn't just rolling in from my modeling. Shortly thereafter, I started working as security as well. It all just kind of went hand in hand. Personal training, modeling, and security all require quite a bit of physical endurance, and of course, vanity had its place. I bounced between the three for several years, before finally realizing that I had to settle into one of them and really make my mark. This would be difficult to decide, because I've always been fortunate enough to do the things that I loved and that I was good at, so none of them ever really seemed like work. In the end I realized that my passion was for personal training—precisely because it was so personal. Personal for me, and personal for all those folks whose lives I would become an intimate part of. I loved the idea of training from the moment I started doing it. There's an unexplainable satisfaction that comes from educating someone about something they can do to truly change their life. That notion had me hooked! It's an ability that's empowering, liberating, yet very humbling. I've seen countless individuals live out their dreams of taking control of their lives, and not just in the gym, but at home and in the office. I would not trade that experience for anything in the world.

Our physical well-being is the most important gift we possess. God only gives us one body, so it's our responsibility to take care of it. We are physical creatures by nature, and our ability to endure physical challenges has always been a benchmark for a man's prowess. Whatever you do, please use the knowledge in this piece to help yourself get physically fit.

Your approach to this lifestyle adjustment should be very personal, and specific to you. Well-informed advice should be welcomed, but ultimately the decisions you make should be based on your best interest and specific to your goals. If you need assistance in achieving your personal goals for becoming the best you can physically possibly be, I would suggest that you seek the instruction of a certified personal fitness trainer. The ACSM (the American College of Sports Medicine) certifies trainers on an international level, and there are many other reputable certifying agencies that are authorized on a national and state level, from which PFTs receive their training. Basically, PFTs should be able to educate you on the proper use of fitness equipment, the proper form and technique for each exercise, as well as proper stretching and warm-up techniques. They should also work with you to create an exercise regimen that best suits your fitness level, and short- and long-term goals.

But if a PFT is not in your future, or in your budget for that matter, don't be discouraged. I'm about to tell you some of the secrets that I have used for more than two decades to achieve my objectives, as well as to help others achieve their goals for a physically fit life.

CHECK YOURSELF

One of the most important steps as you begin taking control of your physical well-being is to arm yourself with knowledge. Yes, that means seeing a physician on a regular basis—at least once a year. Having an annual physical exam is the only way to ensure that everything in your body is functioning properly. Your doctor can also help advise you on a safe exercise program. We as Black males have developed a very real fear of physicians, but trust me when I tell you that that fear of the unknown pales in comparison to the unknown illness you may have that can kill you. You owe it to yourself, and everyone else you care about, and who cares about you, to go see a doctor.

In the event that you do not have health insurance, and cannot afford a doctor's visit, you can go to the main intake area of a network of hospitals (in New York, it is the HHC, the New York City Health and Hospitals Corporation) and they will walk you through the process of getting a free or very low-cost physical exam by a physician at that network facility. The process doesn't take that long, but it is priceless.

In addition to the general physical exam, Black and Latino males should ask and expect the physician to give them a very clear explanation of their blood pressure and diabetes status. There should be a series of blood tests done (which requires that a reasonable amount of your blood be drawn and sent to a laboratory to be tested). The test should consist of, but not be limited to, a hemogram, a comprehensive metabolic panel, and a fasting lipid panel. It is recommended that Black and Latino men begin having an annual prostate (cancer) examination at age forty. It has been stated that the age is fifty, but given the current national weight crisis, among these groups forty is a far safer age to begin this very important annual ritual.

Be sure to express every health concern that you have, or have had, to the physician. Any concern that you have, he or she should either be able to relieve that concern and/or take the necessary steps to address and treat it.

If you have or are engaging in unsafe and unprotected sex, you must get tested for all sexually transmitted diseases including HIV/AIDS. With HIV/AIDS, it is best not to have sex for three months after the unprotected sex, then get tested. That is because it takes about three months for HIV to show up in your bloodstream. To avoid all this unnecessary stress, please be sure to always use a lubricated latex condom or, better yet, abstain from sex altogether, since this is the age of AIDS. Sex, like food that is not good for you, can be an addiction, one that can kill you, literally. So think long and hard about who you partner with, do *not* partner with anyone not willing to share their complete sexual history with you, and understand the difference between love and sex. And please do *not* have multiple sex partners, whether you are using a condom or not. It is spiritually dirty and sexually irresponsible.

PLEASE UNDERSTAND THAT THE INFORMATION THAT YOU DISCUSS WITH ANY MEDICAL PROFESSIONAL (NURSE, DOCTOR, ETC.) HAS TO, BY LAW, BE HELD IN THE STRICTEST OF CONFIDENTIALITY (PRIVACY). SO DO NOT WITHHOLD ANY INFORMATION OR CONCERNS THAT YOU MAY HAVE, WHETHER MEDICAL OR PHYSICAL.

You might be surprised that sometimes what seems like the smallest thing is an indicator of something far bigger, and some of the biggest things are indicators of the smallest. This is best assessed by a medical professional.

I will share, very briefly, a medical experience that I had last year. At first it seemed it might be devastatingly life-altering, but then turned out to be an adjustment that I consciously made, with my best interest at hand. However, I wound up having to change it right back!

As my medical and physical history will indicate, I am in pretty good, no—dare I say—*impeccable*, condition, as I have been monitoring and maintaining my health for over twenty-five years. At the beginning of 2007, I decided that I didn't need to work out as much as I had been doing over the course of those twenty-five years, so I scaled my four to five days a week back to two to three days. Little did I know that my body had become extremely comfortable with that degree of physical expectation, and the reduction of exercise resulted in multiple symptoms and indicators of a form of RA (rheumatoid arthritis), an autoimmune disease that causes severe pain, swelling, stiffness, and discomfort in various joints about your body. It can be treated, but not yet cured. And it gets progressively worse.

After several months of tests, and ever-increasing and sometimes excruciating pain and inflammation, I told my physician about the change I made in my regimen. Then I told the rheumatology specialist who, after several more tests, suggested that my symptoms were probably caused by the changes I made in my workout routine. He directed me to immediately return to my years-old practices, and the symptoms rapidly subsided. They haven't resurfaced either in more than a year of follow-ups and assessments. All of which is to say that sometimes it's not what you do but, as in my case, what you don't do, or stop doing.

Next you need to make a very realistic assessment of where you are physically, and then envision exactly where you would like to be. Try to be as ruthless and uncompromising as you can, but remember that not everybody has to be a bodybuilder or a male model. Whatever your body type, your biggest priority should be to live a long, healthy life, and enjoy it to the fullest.

Most people fall into one of two general body types, so before

planning your fitness program, ask yourself: Are you an ectomorph or an endomorph? The ectomorph body type has a lean,
thin build. Their metabolism burns calories at a rapid rate and
they struggle to keep weight on. In order for the ectomorph to
gain weight, the muscle cells must be stimulated through weight
training. On the other hand, the endomorph is known for natural
body bulk. Their bodies metabolize calories at a slow rate, so the
endomorph must maintain a diet low in fat with a medium-to-
low carbohydrate intake (but not below 100 grams of carbohy-
drates a day). Aerobic work along with a structural weight-training
program is a must to lower an endomorph's body fat. Nutritional
supplements can also enhance the metabolism. Realize that if you
are in poor physical condition, it probably took you a fairly long
time to get to that point. Correcting that will not be an overnight
process—but it is still very attainable. But first you have to get
your mind right. This is where that self-discipline I learned in the
navy comes in handy. You have to "commit yourself to yourself,"
and make some sacrifices. These may be changes in your diet, eating habits, sleeping habits, and working habits.

DRINK MORE WATER

Our bodies are made mostly of water, yet few people drink enough
of it. Many times when you feel tired or cranky you are actually
dehydrated. Everybody should be consuming three to four gal-
lons of water a week. That may sound like a lot, but spread out
over the course of an entire week, it's not that difficult. Make sure
the water is available in small containers at the various locations
where you spend your day.

EAT METHODICALLY

Your body is methodical, in the sense that it bases its activities on the schedule you establish. Of course we're not *mechanical*—there can be some variance—but you should eat at fairly regular periods during the day, so that your body knows when it will receive the fuel necessary to power your machine. Schedule your meals, at least 5 to 6 small ones, at roughly the same time each day, so your body knows what to expect. *Do not* eat based on hunger, but instead eat small meals (portions about the size of your clinched fist) at each of these five to six intervals, so that your body will become used to having the fuel available, to power its daily activities as they arise. In other words, eat for what you are about to do, as opposed to what you have done. What we sometimes perceive to be "hunger" could really be just us seeking a psychological reward.

ELIMINATE FAST FOOD!

And that's not just McDonald's, Burger King, and KFC, but Golden Krust and your local Chinese food joint, too! Fast food is *anything* that's prepared in "mass quantity" for "mass consumption" in *most* public facilities. These items are most always high in *sodium* as well as MSG or monosodium glutamate, a preservative that lengthens the amount of time these items can remain in sellable condition, and *saturated fat*, the worst kind of fat for your heart and arteries.

Instead of running to the corner store when you are hungry, set aside some time during the week to prepare some medium to large quantities of food—at home, in a healthy manner. Bake or roast a whole chicken or turkey, along with some brown rice or whole wheat pasta. Package it in Ziplocs or Tupperware for daily transport to work and the gym. Getting into this habit allows you to have your meals readily available for the eating schedule I mentioned earlier.

STAY FRESH

Substitute fresh fruit and raw vegetables for those items that are displayed near the exits of most bodegas and convenience stores. Most of those items are highly indigestible because of the many artificial (fake) ingredients they contain, and the staggering amounts of sugar and sodium in them. I am talking about candy, cakes, and potato chips. Eliminate them all from your diet over time. Fresh fruits are "travel-sized" for a reason: so that you can keep them readily available at all times.

MORE SIMPLE FOOD TIPS

- Never skip meals when you are trying to lose weight. Your metabolism's clock is based on your eating schedule, and skipping meals disrupts that clock. When the body is deprived of regularly scheduled meals, a natural defense mechanism engages to store fat for future use. In these cases, your body will burn muscle before fat.
- Lighter and smaller meals (snacks) are for less active times. These snacks can and should include fresh fruit—pears, apples (both green and red), pineapples, oranges, and bananas.
- When grocery shopping—which is much better and

cheaper than eating out—be aware of the fat, sugar, and sodium levels in all the foods you select. Whole grains are better than processed white flour. Wheat pasta is better than macaroni. Buy fresh fruit and vegetables in small portions so they don't go bad.

FIBER FIBER FIBER!

Anyone who has talked to me for more than five minutes about physical fitness knows that I am a staunch advocate of the use of both supplemental and dietary fiber. Your body does not literally process fiber, but the daily consumption of fiber assists in maximizing your body's digestive process, reduces the retention of excess fat cells, and normalizes bowel movements. Begin with one teaspoon, twice daily (morning/evening) of a dietary fiber (e.g., Benefiber), then eventually increase to one tablespoon, twice daily, of the same. Additionally, take at least one serving of a soluble fiber supplement (e.g., Metamucil) once a week.

DON'T SLEEP ON SLEEP

You prioritize work, making sure you get there on time, do your work and sometimes the work of others, and never hesitate to stay late. All for the check, whether it is to pay the bills, buy the stuff you want, or to take care of the family. Do the same for sleep—it's critical for your body to recover and repair itself. All the reasons you prioritize work, apply to why you should make it your business to get seven to eight hours of sleep each day (and if you can't get it all in at night, a brief nap at some point during the day never hurts). Few of us get enough rest, which messes with our metabolism, our mental function, and our overall wellness.

That's why this will not be an overnight process: we're talking about lifestyle changes that you must commit yourself to for the rest of your life. It's those repetitive, habitual practices that become the foundation for who you are. Healthy habits will lead to a healthier you.

TAKE TIME

No excuses. If you can't take the time, make the time. Thirty minutes of exercise per day is better than none at all, so don't set yourself up to fail by thinking that it's an hour or it's nothing. Nor should you deceive yourself to think that exercising nonstop will make you fit. Your body needs more rest than it does exercise, because our muscles need time to repair themselves.

To begin, I suggest that you exercise, vigorously, for no less than thirty minutes or more than sixty minutes, on three separate occasions, weekly. Allow at least a one-day interval in between sessions for your body to adjust and recover. Maintain this regimen for at least six months before making any adjustments to time frame or number of days. This is a lifestyle change, and your body will need that period to adapt to a regular routine.

But exercise is not all about getting ripped. First and foremost, exercise is the best way to ensure that you live a long, healthy, and productive life. Please understand that that applies to everyone reading this. And please be clear about what is considered exercise. The definition of exercise is to *exert*, to put to use one's power or influence. And that's exactly what you have to do, use your God-given power over your mind and body to effect a positive change and increase the functionality of your entire body.

Exercise increases stamina, strength, resistance to illness, mental sharpness, and a host of other aspects of daily life. As Black males we are given our history and cultural traditions, and we are capable of assuming and maintaining a lifestyle that will perpetuate a lengthy and productive life. There are several specific, simple, and sometimes not-so-simple things we can do in our daily routines to help ourselves become healthier individuals. Not only for our own good but to be an example to all those younger Black males who will see us, and want to be us.

WALK A LITTLE MORE

Take the stairs instead of the elevator. Take the local train, get off a stop or two before your stop, and walk—briskly—the rest of the way home. Turn off that TV and get outside. You might be amazed at the difference that a brisk walk can make in your mental and muscular functions—especially your heart muscle. Notice that I emphasized brisk. The stroll is not gonna cut it! Best of all is a quick pace for a sustained period of time or specific distance, which you gradually increase over the days and weeks. Simply put, walk it out three times a week, a little bit longer and a little bit farther every time.

PUSH WEIGHT

Challenge your body to work a little harder for you with some resistance training. Whether it's at your local gym, or in your living room, take the time to learn how to perform a routine of resistance (weight-lifting) exercises to acclimate your body to doing more than it is used to. No, you don't have to join a fancy health club. The YMCA offers very cost-effective gym facilities throughout the country. Memberships are inexpensive, and they even offer discounts and assistance for individuals and families who need it.

EXPECT HIGH EXPECTATIONS

Exercise prompts you to have expectations of yourself, and allows you to have them of others. If you have a partner, get him or her involved in your workout plan. An exercise buddy is the next best thing to a personal trainer. You can feed off each other's energy, and push each other to the limit. You can't beat the appreciation you are going to have for each other, and the benefits you will both reap, from having a healthier and happier partner and a long life together.

In retrospect, I saved the best and the worst for last. If you implement and adhere to at least half the information and advice contained in this essay, you are on your way to being at least better than you were yesterday. And adding days and years to your tomorrows. But I would be remiss if I did not strongly suggest that you reduce considerably, if not just completely eliminate, your use of controlling substances (beer, liquor, cigars, cigarettes, marijuana, speed, LSD, cocaine, heroin, and all other forms of physical, mental, and social disablers). The use of any or all of those substances is severely detrimental to your overall well-being, but especially so when you are asking your body to perform above its actual capabilities when you have crippled it with any of these drugs. There is no such thing as the recreational use of any of these substances—recreation is a time of leisure and play. This body, this machine, is a one of a kind, and it is the only one you will get, and is always at work! Embrace your lives, and take control of how long you will be a productive member of the fraternity that we are, Black Men!

6

Moving Toward Mental Wellness

By Andraé L. Brown, Ph.D.

As I write this, my father is in the hospital, having just suffered his fourth heart attack in ten years. I remember when I got the call. I had just finished working twelve hours and was completely exhausted when my wife phoned. Trying to sound calm, she asked: "Did you talk to your mother?"

"No," I replied. "Why, what's up?"

"Well, your dad just had a heart attack," she said. "Actually, he had a heart attack this morning and they just decided to call the ambulance this evening. He is in the VA hospital in Durham." I was silent. "Are you all right?" my wife asked, interrupting my far-away thoughts. My mind was traveling back twenty-one years to the days when I was eleven and my dad had his first "heart attack." I vividly recall the time when we were in the recreation room in our home in upstate New York and my dad, a big, strapping six-foot-three-inch man, just buckled to one knee like an oak tree chopped at the base. As he kneeled, wincing and clutching his chest, I repeatedly asked him what was wrong. He simply said: "I'm all right. Go get me some water." Just like the soldier he had been in Vietnam, he put on his game face and waited it out. He never went to the hospital, never had a follow-up visit with his doctor. In fact, he never even received a medical diagnosis as to what really happened on that unforgettable day in Newburgh, New York. From my years of life, and my professional experience, I am now convinced that he had a heart attack.

Seven years later, I was eighteen and a sophomore in college when I received a frantic call from my mother saying that dad had had "another" heart attack. My younger brother and I immediately drove from college straight to the hospital. Four hours and three hundred miles later, I was face-to-face with my dad. This brawny man lay prostrate on a hospital bed that seemed too small for a man of his stature, with an infinite amount of tubes and wires protruding from his chest while his entire family stood around. For the first time in my life he appeared mortal (well, almost). Fortunately, he recovered quickly. Like a true soldier, he willed himself to health and returned to his pastoral duties as a Pentecostal preacher within a week.

Over the next ten years, this same pattern would emerge, and each time he made it a point to walk out of the hospital. As he saw it, heart attacks and strokes were minor setbacks; he would always live to fight another day. My father's fight was not against flesh and blood but against the dark forces of the world. New combatants emerged daily, whether racism, sexism, corruption, police brutality, domestic violence, addictions, and the challenges of raising a family of seven children—and he battled them all with great vigilance.

These experiences with my father's health helped me to recognize that there is a direct correlation between mental health, physical health, and oppression. Whenever my dad's condition deteriorated, I knew that my life could change dramatically, and my mental health suffered as a result.

Like most people faced with the reality of losing a parent, I was constantly on edge and anxious. I got depressed, and there were times I thought I would lose my mind. Ever since the age of eleven, following my father's first cardiac episode, I began preparing to step into a leadership role in case he died. The psychological strain was tremendous. While there were no formal discussions or quorums, I believed it was my responsibility, as the oldest son, to take care of the family in case of emergency. Because of these and other life-altering events, I began a long-term battle with depression. I became preoccupied with and, at the same time, desensitized to death and my own mortality. I also became what some might consider a workaholic and overly responsible.

The result was double-edged: great achievements at a young age, coupled with significant stress. It has taken me many years to work through these issues, thanks to prayer, self-exploration, and therapy. Still, maintaining my sanity and making sense of this world is a daily struggle. Every week, I realize there are unexplored parts of my life, some of them I avoid like the plague until I build up the courage to face them; but as I do, my life becomes more fulfilling and meaningful.

Most fathers, be they good or bad, are models of manhood in their sons' eyes. Watching my father navigate the world as a Pentecostal preacher, tasting all of its joys and disappointments, battling his personal demons while providing spiritual and earthly guidance to our family, church, and community, influenced my personal and career choices. I was not "called" to be a preacher. Instead, my ministry is to serve as a professor, psychologist, family therapist, school counselor, and social justice advocate. It is from this perspective that I explore critical issues in developing and maintaining mental health for Black males. Although some people are ashamed to talk about mental health, our physical health and mental wellness are deeply interconnected, and both are vitally important for bolstering resilience in Black males.

Defining Mental Health

Although Black males experience mental health crises all the time, discussions of mental health have been historically a taboo subject in the Black community. A combination of factors—racism, substance abuse, poverty, homophobia, stress and anxiety, domestic and community trauma, incarceration, and dismantled families, to name a few—take their toll on our mental and physical health, with a resulting decline in life expectancy, education, and income levels. Black males are marked by poor mental health outcomes compared to men and boys from other ethnic or racial groups. When we do seek help, there is a high risk for receiving poor-quality mental health services, which is partially due to the lack of proficient mental health providers trained to deal with people from culturally, ethnically, racially, and sexually diverse backgrounds.

There are many misconceptions about what constitutes mental health. Former U.S. surgeon general Dr. David Satcher described mental health as the successful performance of mental functions resulting in productive activities, fulfilling relationships, the ability to adapt to change, and successfully coping with adversity. When an individual is unable to function effectively, we need a better understanding of their mental health.

Mental illness comes from a variety of factors. Some individuals are born with severe and intense emotional, cognitive, and mental deficits such as fetal alcohol syndrome or genetic disorders such as Down syndrome. Others may develop Alzheimer's disease as they mature. Some illnesses remain dormant only to be exacerbated by instability in one's physical, emotional, and mental states.

Mental health issues can occur in all families, and in every generation. Knowing someone's family history plays a critical role in understanding and treating mental illness. But it's more important to know how one's family responds to mental health issues than whether mental illness is a part of the family structure.

In my work with clients, I have found that some psychological pain results from intense internal conflicts. These may come from an absence of structure, experiences of loss, or a desire for a spiritual direction. Drug addictions, adverse medical treatments, misdiagnoses, reactions to traumatic events, and economic and emotional oppression are all issues that can affect one's mental state. Oftentimes, the psychological discomfort people endure is a direct reaction to the community, cultural, and political systems to which they belong. Sadly, many people are labeled mentally ill when they are merely responding to extraordinarily challenging social conditions.

While mental disorders may be more common than most people realize, the good news is they are treatable. This may occur through individual, group, and family therapy. Also, when there is a biological basis for the impairment, medication is an option. Unfortunately, many Black males choose to "self-medicate" to cope with their symptoms and mask their underlying hurts before seeking professional help. This self-medication may take the form of risky sexual practices and behavior, violence, drugs, alcohol, self-mutilation, and eating disorders (yes, Black males do suffer from bulimia and anorexia).

While many Black males will rationalize their use of marijuana, for instance, as a cultural, medicinal, or spiritual practice, it is more commonly a sedative to waylay one's anxieties and pain. Consequently, individuals who self-medicate with mind-altering substances develop dual diagnoses. What occurs is a "boomerang" effect—men begin to use substances to cope with the problems and in return develop an addiction. Subsequently, they have to address both the substance abuse and mental health issues in treatment.

Whatever issues one faces, it is critically important that the negative stigma associated with mental health be replaced by life-affirming and empowering treatments. In order to accomplish this, we must understand the complexity of Black males, their thinking, motivations, and actions. That's why it is impossible to talk about Black men's and Black boys' mental health and wellness without dealing with issues of race, gender, sexual orientation, age, and class.

Mental, Physical, and Spiritual Health

While everyone's journey toward mental health is unique, there are a few common concepts that must be kept in mind. All aspects of our health—mental, physical, and spiritual—are intimately linked. It is a fallacy to think that a person can compartmentalize, or separate their different identities and roles in the world. If a person is balanced psychologically, the chances of maintaining a healthy physical and spiritual life increase. Similarly, if a problem exists in one of these areas, it is likely that there will be problems in other areas. For example, while my father focused on recuperating from a heart attack, he did not concentrate on his mental health. Similarly, if one feels spiritually disconnected and isolated, believing no one cares about them, they will not be physically or psychologically strong because their soul is hurting. One of the keys to maintaining mental wellness is to strive toward fulfilling all aspects of one's life—the mental, the physical, and the spiritual. Balancing all three increases the likelihood of leading a healthy and successful life. However, many of us Black males do ourselves a disservice by neglecting our physical and mental health. Such damaging choices hurt us as well as the people who care about us most—and the Black community as a whole.

Black Males and Therapy

One of the biggest myths in psychology is that Black males are averse to therapy. Both patients and practitioners buy into this dangerous misconception. In fact, I have found that once Black men and Black boys engage in treatment with people who they feel are skilled, understanding, and truly care about them, they are committed to the process.

In my practice we maintain an open system, encouraging clients to return after their initial therapeutic goals have been met. It is not uncommon for our clients—both court-ordered and volunteers—to bring friends and family members to therapy with them for support in their journey toward healing and transformation. Some of our most challenging and resistant clients have made glowing referrals and recommendations to their friends and family to participate in therapy. I once told a colleague who was unable to engage a young Black male in treatment, "He has no problem with talking. He just chooses not to talk to you." I implored him to build rapport, gain the client's trust, and be genuine. Most importantly, he had to create a safe, intimate environment in which the young man could disclose his innermost thoughts and fears and challenges. Once this environment is created, Black males lose their "cool pose," allow themselves to be vulnerable, and initiate the healing process.

As Black males we must understand that maintaining mental health is a communal responsibility, not just an individual effort. Mental health ties directly into the psychological, emotional, and physical liberation of all people. In working with Black men and Black boys, I always situate our experiences in a familial, social, political, cultural, and historical context. I find that this approach affirms and restores our clients' humanity—and raises the critical consciousness needed to deal with oppressive social structures. Instead of focusing on immediate and private distress, I try to view the clients' predicaments as a communal experience requiring a collective response. This teaches new coping mechanisms for future crises, and tends to offset the challenges inherent in capitalism, patriarchy, and White supremacy. This communal approach is analogous to a goal-line defense in football. The aim is to fortify and protect the goal line while simultaneously attacking the offense.

As Black men and Black boys we must engage in intense dialogues about how we use unearned privileges to oppress others. Like it or not, we enjoy certain undeserved benefits from being male. For example, in traditional, heterosexual, dual-income relationships, household chores are typically the responsibility of women and girls. We need to shift this line of thinking and start sharing in duties without being asked to do so. On a global scale, men receive higher salaries and have more opportunities for advancement in the workplace than their female counterparts.

For healing to occur it is imperative that Black males take accountability for our missteps and develop strategies to repair the hurt caused by our overt and covert abuses of power. When we take a proactive approach to solving our problems, we empower ourselves and bolster our overall resilience to all of life's challenges.

Recognizing Everyday Trauma

Much of my clinical work, teaching, and training with community organizations has focused on trauma. Psychological or emotional trauma—often involving the threat of death or serious bodily injury—invokes a sense of horror, powerlessness, and helplessness. The experience of trauma may be environmental (community violence or domestic violence) or personal (witnessing or experiencing assault or abuse). It can be chronic or result from a single event, such as Hurricane Katrina.

Two people exposed to the same event can respond and interpret it very differently. This is most commonly seen among siblings. A traumatic event, such as the loss of a parent, may serve as motivation for one sibling, while the other child is completely devastated and takes years to recover. Well-known traumatic events, such as the 9/11 attacks, Hurricane Katrina, and the Virginia Tech massacre, are sometimes easier for people to understand because of all the publicity that arouses public empathy and a desire to help.

But there are many everyday disasters that go unnoticed, underreported, or simply do not register as traumatic because they seem so common. For instance, the single mother who learns her son has been killed in street violence is dealing with trauma. The young kid who finds his dad's gun under the bed and accidentally shoots his neighbor suffers as well. The young high school student infected with HIV is experiencing trauma. So is the boy who develops a stuttering problem or incontinence because he is abruptly removed from his home and school due to neglect or abuse. The teenager suffering from insomnia because he is being intimidated into joining a gang is suffering trauma, just like the husband who loses his job and starts beating his wife in front of his children. Other daily offenses include illness, imprisonment, police violence, living with alcoholism and addiction, and all the adverse conditions of poverty. As I work with people struggling to maintain a healthy mental balance, these are examples of what I call "unappreciated traumas," or circumstances that are less likely to be considered—and treated as—traumatic.

Unfortunately, these are precisely the sorts of situations that many Black males deal with daily. In fact, Black men and Black boys are in dire need of mental health services to address trauma. This need for accurate mental health assessments and effective treatments is not an indication of increased pathology among Black males, but rather a reflection of their vulnerability in society. Still, their feeling of being overwhelmed is generally overlooked. Indeed, chronic exposure to these traumatic events can change the brain's chemistry and have an enormous impact on behavior. Symptoms of trauma may include increased physical, emotional, and psychological anxiety. Males may also reexperience trauma through invasive memories, dreams, and flashbacks. Some experience emotional numbing and avoidance, whereby they seem depressed, closed off, or shut down, refusing to discuss anything associated with the event. Fortunately, researchers have found that therapeutic intervention can slow down and reverse these effects.

The most susceptible youth are young people from neighborhoods with high rates of female-headed households living below the poverty level, and low school attendance and employment rates. Research suggests, and my personal experience confirms, that up to 50 percent of youth involved in the justice system meet the criteria for post-traumatic stress disorder (PTSD). This rate is up to eight times higher than in the general population. For instance, maltreated children (those experiencing abuse and neglect) are 59 percent more likely to be arrested before they reach age eighteen, and 30 percent more likely to be arrested for violent crime. Furthermore, 92 percent of youth involved in the juvenile justice system report some type of trauma, which then can result in hyperactivity, inability to pay attention, extreme impulsiveness, aggression, anger, paranoia, aloofness, and the inability to develop close relationships. In many instances, these young people are involved in the mental health system, but their direct and vicarious traumas have never been addressed. Worse, many are misdiagnosed and their responses to psychological trauma are pathologized to a degree whereby they are diverted from the mental health system and ushered directly into the prison-industrial complex.

Our failure to encourage young Black men to focus on their mental health has left many of them unaware of the impact of their life choices. This lack of information and resources makes them more reluctant to address their mental health challenges. This attitude is often transferred into the mantra many men adopt, that "whatever does not kill me will make me stronger." Although necessary for survival, this resilient attitude also has its repercussions.

Residuals of Trauma

Like many who serve in the armed forces, my father has suffered the physical and psychological effects of war. Many of his physical ailments are unofficially connected to his exposure to malaria and chemical agents while in Vietnam. Though he has long been under a doctor's care for high blood pressure, kidney failure, heart attacks, strokes, gout, asthma, and hypertension, he has just begun to address the symptoms of post-traumatic stress disorder with a mental health professional at the VA hospital. For the previous twenty-seven years, his way of dealing with this situation was through spirituality. As a child, I recall hearing him recount from the pulpit nights when he lay in bed dreaming of shooting laser beams from his eyes to defend him from what appeared to be demons filling the room. He thought that if he did not kill all of the demons he would not wake up. These nightmares were accompanied by sleepless nights, cold sweats, body jerking, and other visceral reactions. As a minister, he viewed these "sightings" in a spiritual way, and the church parishioners related them to a struggle between good and evil. Whether viewed as a spiritual battle or a psychological disorder, he and our whole family shared in this suffering for most of our lives. But since beginning therapy and joining a veteran support group, my father has learned better coping strategies and experienced some relief.

The entire family rests better knowing that he no longer suffers this sort of pain. My mother in particular does not have to worry as much before going to bed. But I often imagine what our lives might have been like if he had addressed these issues thirty years ago. How much more peaceful, productive, and emotionally available might he have been? Would he have been more receptive and trusting of the medical profession if he had been properly diagnosed back then?

Even today, my father is uncomfortable disclosing his mental health history with his doctors. Fortunately he talks to me, but I must constantly remind him that receiving support does not mean there is something wrong with him. He is simply reacting to trauma, a part of his life that needs addressing. I reassure him that he is more of a man for confronting his emotional needs and seeking the healing he deserves. But he believes that his pain is some sort of punishment for engaging in war. This pain is a constant reminder of the most horrific period of his life. And the disappointment and racism he experienced when he returned to his home in small-town North Carolina after his tour of duty are also connected to his trauma. Millions of homeless, drug addicted, and mentally ill soldiers—young and old—share his pain. But like him, they can reauthor their lives.

My father occasionally wears a veteran's hat. He has visited the Vietnam War Memorial in Washington, D.C., to participate in Memorial Day and Veterans Day ceremonies. These visits are major milestones in his life, an integral part of his healing process. As the Iraq War persists, and more soldiers return to civilian life after serving multiple tours of duty, it will be imperative for our communities—whether through the church or through grassroots organizations—to ensure that these veterans make a healthy transition back into society.

The Legacy and Impact of Violence

In the 1988 film *Tongues Untied*, filmmaker Marlon Riggs eloquently illustrates the emotional roller coaster many Blacks experience, in the form of a chant: "Anger unvented becomes pain, unspoken becomes rage, released becomes violence. . . ." Too often, the focus is placed on anger, temper, rage, and violence instead of the unspoken pain at the root of the problem. The problem is complicated by the fact that most people have neither the language nor the arena to express their emotions. Parents of adolescents struggle with understanding their sons' behavior as they shift from expressing a full range of emotions to displaying only what parents perceive as anger. Parental complaints range from "What's really wrong with him?" "Why is he so angry?" "He is a good person, but he has such a bad temper," "He gets so frustrated when he can't express himself that he can't contain himself," to "He's just plain mean!"

The same observations apply to adult men who have not yet developed the *skills* to express their full range of emotions. For some this lack of expression is learned behavior. For example, we spank children and then tell them not to cry. At that moment they are physically, emotionally, and spiritually wounded, they are not allowed to express themselves. So they suck up their tears and turn the frown into a scowl. Eventually, they may skip the crying and go directly to the scowl. These perceived bad tempers may be reactions to everyday traumas including racism, sexism, and domestic violence. Many adult men are still scowling and "sucking it up," whether they are aware of it or not. Some have begun to define themselves by the emotions they wear on their sleeves. Others are self-aware but can't push through the wall without more support.

Many males seek anger management as a way to address these issues. While anger management provides some relief, managing anger so it does not explode into violence is different than addressing the underlying issues of the anger. Many people seek individual, family, or group counseling in order to probe deeper and "unpack the baggage" they may be carrying around.

Like many Black males, I come from *a legacy of violence* that penetrates all my family relationships and colors the lens through which I view the world. As a child, I did not know much about my parents' upbringing. When other kids would talk about going to their grandparents' house, I could not relate. My father's mother died of a heart attack, and an arsonist murdered his dad. In fact, my father was in the house when it was set ablaze. He is the only survivor of the fire. My only two memories of my maternal grandmother are of her sleeping, and then at her funeral. As for my maternal grandfather, he was just dead. Whenever I pressed my mom for details about his death, her typical response—"You always ask too many questions"—shut down the conversation.

I gained some insight into her life when I came across a newspaper clipping she stored in the family safe, also known as "the big white Bible." An article from the local newspaper, titled "Love Triangle Results in the Death of Asheboro Negro," described the death of my grandfather and the attempted murder of his lover. Reading that brief clipping, I learned that my grandfather begged his girlfriend Maggie to release the peace order (restraining order) and when she agreed and turned away to walk in the house, he shot her in the back, then blew his head off with a shotgun. Beside him were two notes. One said: "I killed Maggie and I'm going with her." The second said: "We must be together in hell. Please don't cry."

After reading this small scrap of worn paper, I lay in bed and cried like a baby. I wept for my grandfather, for Maggie and her family. I cried for my mother, both as a little girl (just six at the time of the incident) and as the grown woman who still endures this pain. I was nineteen years old when I learned how my grandfather died, and only then could I finally begin to understand the intense and volatile nature of my family, and of the community where we lived. I recognized that although families might migrate in search of better opportunities, the residual effects of trauma and violence stay with us. My family came from a place in the South where Black people kill Black people and White police cross the tracks to pick up bodies. As in many poor and working-class Black communities, there was no middle ground; it was either heaven or hell, right or wrong. Unless you were doing something completely positive, your life could revolve around drinking, fighting, shooting, and having babies.

I initially understood my grandfather's story to be about violence in the Black community. I later recognized that it was not just a "Black thing." Unfortunately, it reflects the all-too-common experience of women who try to leave abusive relationships and men who feel as if women are objects that they can exert control over, or simply destroy. Even today, there is no protection for many women in these types of relationships, just as there was no protection for Maggie back then.

I now understand that love, violence, sex, family, addictions, suffering, pain, religion, and the afterlife are all connected. I know that there is a very thin line between mental health and insanity, between love, caring, compassion, and murder. I wondered, *Did my grandfather ever give off signs that he was suicidal or homicidal?* I wondered if he was mean and abusive to everyone, or did he just snap? Was he addicted to drugs and alcohol? Did anyone ever refer him to get counseling—and if so, would he have gone? I wondered what sort of message his very public, violent death sent to my aunts and uncles about misogyny, sexism, and the value of women. What did they learn about manhood from this tragedy? Who taught and supported them after their father died? What resources did Maggie have? Although a peace order was issued against my grandfather, did the police understand the threat she was under? Because she was "a negress," as the paper describes, did they even care? After learning more about my family history I realized the vulnerability and volatility of my own life. I had within me the potential to be both a victim and a perpetrator of violence. I share this because, while this is my daily struggle, it is the same struggle faced by many other Black males.

Am I My Brother's Keeper?

Why do Black males kill other Black males? When people learn that I am a psychologist who works with families of color and youth who are transitioning from the juvenile justice system, I am often asked this question. Scholars, teachers, preachers, barbers, and street corner philosophers have all tried to figure out this troubling conundrum. Explanations are vast and numerous, but most often get reduced to: Black males are angry and inherently violent. What is often missing from these explanations is the global context, the fact that the perceived violence and rage are an inevitable response to systematic oppression.

Black males do not have a monopoly on violence. We are neither creators nor masters of it. Violence begets violence. Black men and Black boys are violent because the world is violent. Violence permeates every aspect of our existence from domestic violence and schoolyard fights to ethnic cleansing and global wars. People (not just Black males) kill as a way of dominating, controlling, and subordinating another person or group. Violence is perceived as an efficient strategy for conflict resolution because it is easy to implement and because the outcomes of intimidation and death are long-lasting and permanent. The same rules apply on a global scale, among people of all races and classes: first, employ tactics of coercion and persuasion; if that doesn't work, try brutality.

All Black people, across socioeconomic and gender lines, are directly impacted by Black-on-Black violence. Entire communities are destroyed, literally and figuratively. When men use violence, women and children are left vulnerable, unprotected, and required to "pick up the pieces." For our survival as a people, we must stop committing acts of violence and brutality toward one another. And not just for the immediately obvious reasons.

To achieve our goal of mental wellness, it is critical that we begin taking a position of nonviolence in every aspect of our lives, and implementing strategies to promote community-wide healing. This is easier said than done, of course, but it starts by committing yourself to not hurt anyone else. The next step is to choose a lifestyle that avoids situations where violence can occur. When I made a commitment to be nonviolent, in my mid-twenties, I attempted to create a new identity that promoted peace. I began to distance myself from people, places, and things that I associated with violence. My mentality was consistent with Mobb Deep's 1995 song, "Shook Ones Part II": . . . *cause ain't no such things as halfway crooks.* When I made this commitment, I went all in—no guns, no fights, no volatile relationships. I steered clear of parties where I knew there was a potential for something to "pop off." I was more careful about everything I did because I wanted to protect my life. Understand, I was not scared of violence. I was actually far too comfortable with it, which is how I knew I needed to change my patterns. Becoming nonviolent can be a lonely process, but I started recruiting other friends and by being consistent and committed, we created a new social network. It's still a daily struggle, but well worth it because I know I am creating a new legacy for my family.

Suicide: The Quiet Scream

Beyond the traditional Christian belief that says "suicide is a sin," I once regarded people who committed suicide as weak losers. Even though my grandfather killed himself, I considered people who chose suicide to be soft. As a Black male, I knew that the world was hard, but I also felt it was our destiny to engage in physical, psychological, and spiritual warfare. Anyone who committed suicide was a quitter. To me, they had "punked out of life." They were not allowing God to assist in winning the fight.

Despite my family legacy, I maintained this attitude through my early twenties. But after I appeared callous while writing a case study of a suicidal client, my graduate school professor encouraged me to revisit my assumptions about suicide. I immediately blamed the victim, saying that he was selfish and did not think of his family. Now that he was gone, they were forced to live with the shame of having a husband and father who quit. I defended my position by citing scriptures, providing case studies, and articulating my idea of the ethos of manhood. I explained that while we Black men should not kill ourselves, we might kill another Black man—which I justified as self-hatred projected onto another.

The more I spoke, the more I realized how completely off the mark I was. At the time, I did not fully understand the impact my grandfather's death had on me. Even as I write this piece, I am still trying to figure that one out. But through self-evaluation, I realized that Black males do not talk about feelings of weakness, pain, and vulnerability. Instead of exploring and expressing these feelings that may cause significant suffering, we choose to shun people who are in tune with their emotions, and to condemn those who "fall."

I have since made it my mission to educate myself and become more sensitive to the pain my people have endured. In doing so, I have come to realize that suicide is not a cop-out. It's more about the psychic pain and internal conflicts that people feel. Suicide is not an indication of the weakness of the individual who ends his life, but rather an indictment of their extreme circumstances. When a man says, "I am going to kill myself" or "I wish I were dead," he is expressing a sincere belief that life is so horrible that his only escape from the pain is death. Suicidal thoughts reflect a man at his lowest. At that moment, he believes he is in hell. The psychic pain is tremendous and stifling, nearly impossible to express. Suicide brings attention to this situation in a very loud way.

Men who commit suicide come in all shapes and sizes. There is no economic, physical, or geographic profile—they are just men who cannot see any other way out. Some of these men suffer from deep-depressive bouts, sometimes for extended periods, marked by feelings of doom and gloom, despair, hopelessness, and extreme isolation. Suicidal tendencies can also manifest themselves as an elevated mood with a heightened sense of awareness, recklessness, and unusually extreme thought patterns. Men who attempt suicide are more likely to successfully execute their plan as compared to women, because they have greater access to lethal means, especially firearms. Some prefer a simple plan to kill themselves. Others are a bit more creative.

Whether we want to admit it or not, we all know individuals who are suicidal. We refer to their reckless debauchery as eccentric, extravagant, or simply "living on the wild side." The difference is that these people will do things the average guy would never do, and they are not afraid of the consequences, which may include their own demise. Where others pull back, they keep going. Often they take up the banner of indestructibility because they are in prolonged states of mourning. Have you ever heard a friend in a drunken stupor who says things like: "I don't give a @*$#!"; "Nobody cares about me, anyway"; "This life don't mean anything to me any more"; "If I could end it all now and be left alone, I would do it." Have you ever considered that maybe they really mean it?

The Geto Boys' 1991 song "Mind Playing Tricks on Me" offers

one of the most realistic and haunting tales of the psychological despair that leads to suicide. The Houston rap trio's lyrics relay the tales of three men whose lives are crumbling around them. As they meditate on their daily struggles as well as fractured relationships among family, friends, and intimate partners, they contemplate violence against others and themselves. In one verse rapper Scarface confesses:

> *Day by day it's more impossible to cope / I feel like I'm the one that's doing dope /*

The candid experiences that Scarface, Willie D, and Bushwick Bill rap about present a concise explanation of the mental machinations Black males experience when contemplating suicide. This song deeply resonated with me because I can remember being at that same crossroads. As a young man, I felt trapped, disappointed, and isolated from my family and spiritual core. My best friends were going to jail on an almost weekly basis. It seemed like both the good and bad kids were doing horrible things—murder, rape, robbery, and drugs. Many got away with those things, but the ones who were caught received sentences that lasted as long as they had been alive.

I tried to stay out of the streets by focusing on education. After fighting the school to get out of the "slow" classes, I was placed in the academically gifted program. I focused my attention on being smart enough to save myself and help my family and community. Instead of focusing on basketball and getting high each summer, I participated in summer educational enrichment programs, or "nerd camps" as my brother and friends referred to them. My father and I made a deal. "You do your job in school," he said, "and I will do my job and send you to college."

As a graduating senior, my job was almost complete, but my

family was still broke. After several heated discussions, I realized that what he considered a motivational technique to position me for scholarships was just false hope. With several of my friends dead or in jail, I was devastated, lonely, and hurt. Desperate, I considered running away, but I had nowhere to run and no way to get there. I wanted to just sit down and die. I thought about suicide, but I did not want to go to hell. I developed scenarios in which I could be killed by the police (also known as "suicide by cop") or by someone on the streets. I did not carry out those plans because, even in my despair, I refused to ruin the life of another. Still, I was a mess. My mind was definitely playing tricks on me.

After contemplating my limited options—either get a scholarship, or start hustling in the streets—I concluded that my chances for success were roughly equal in both areas. I believed that my intelligence, ingenuity, and work ethic would enable me to navigate either circumstance and survive. One choice would enable me to live in a nonexploitive and life-affirming manner, while the other would lead to death or prison. Realizing that my parents sacrificed their lives trying to raise me, I did not want to do anything to bring shame to their ministry or my six siblings. And I didn't want to break my father's heart. "I was there for the first heart attack," I thought to myself. "I don't want to cause the last." Slowly I got myself together and developed a plan to finance my way through college.

The *H* Word: Homophobia

I do not want to pretend that suicide, depression, and other mental health issues are just passing thoughts that can be resolved with a gut check and a pep talk. Many of these issues extend from a lifetime of feeling marginalized, mistreated, and isolated—as if you do not count or matter in the world. Another reason men contemplate suicide, or experience other mental health issues, is that they are compelled—or coerced—to keep secrets. Secrets come in many forms, whether cheating on a test, infidelity, tax evasion, or the so-called "code of the streets."

Black males learn early in life to keep secrets, receiving messages from their parents like "Whatever goes on in this house, stays in this house." This mantra carries over and is applied to every aspect of our lives, particularly around issues of sexuality. For example, many gay, bisexual, and transgender Black males feel compelled to deny their sexual identity or keep it a closely guarded secret. As a result, they keep all sorts of complex and competing thoughts and feelings bottled up in a vain attempt to bury their truth inside.

For many queer Black men and boys, feelings of vulnerability and invisibility are commonplace. They may feel as if they do not matter because the world operates under a heterosexual assumption. When a straight person walks in a room their natural inclination is to suppose that everyone in the room is straight. Only when straight people receive evidence to the contrary do they acknowledge those with a different sexual orientation.

A major factor in people maintaining these secrets is homophobia—fear or hatred toward gays, lesbians, bisexual, and transgender people. Another aspect of homophobia is the fear of maintaining intimate relationships with men. Homophobia runs so deep that it can affect the relationships of fathers and their male sons—partially explaining why fathers and sons stop hugging, kissing, and showing affection to each other during early adolescence. In an effort to teach young boys how to be a man who is "tough, independent, and self-reliant," fathers deny intimate, meaningful connections, which often results in young men who are aggressive, emotionally disconnected, and unable to establish supportive relationships with others.

When reflecting on homophobia and its impact on mental health, I'm often reminded of my childhood friend Chris (not his real name). Growing up, everyone knew that Chris was a little different. He was always "extra," whether it was the way he wore his clothes, spoke in class, or chose to style his high-top fade with an additional twist. Whenever we played football, he was always in the house, hanging out with his sister. People in our circle would make remarks about his sexual orientation, but that didn't really mean much—we made horrible jokes about everyone's sexual orientation. Like most adolescent males we were highly intolerant of anything different. Some of the guys taunted and teased him mercilessly. Understanding the politics of this practice, Chris would reluctantly join in as a preemptive strike—and he was quick-witted. But when all else failed, he knew how to fight.

After high school I lost touch with Chris for several years, but when we did reconnect it was via an email advertising his hair salon. In the advertisement, Chris was now "Christi." I had heard he had a hair shop, but I didn't know that he was now a she. Over the next few days, my childhood friends and I discussed this news over email and phone. The tone of the discussions was genuinely positive in our own warped way. Most of my friends were shocked, surprised, "freaked out," relieved but at the same time proud of his/her entrepreneurial success. But really, how are you supposed to react when your homeboy is now a five-foot-seven-inch transgender man with hazel eyes, long flowing locks, and cleavage?

I called Christi and began to reestablish our long-lost friendship. I really did not care if she wanted to be called Chris or Christi, I was just happy to see that my friend was doing well. So many young men and women who are unable to express their sexuality commit suicide, or else turn to drugs, violence, and life on the streets. I still slip up at times and refer to her as a "him," but the more we talk the more comfortable I am with "her." As Christi explained it to me, she is a preoperation transgender man, meaning that she receives hormone treatments and has breast implants, but has not undergone a complete sex change.

I am genuinely pleased that Christi has shown so much resilience and integrity in being who she wants to be. She is creating a life and a family that is her own. Christi has even adopted a young boy whom she is raising with the help of her brother and sister. Christi has weathered so many storms, some of which I am beginning to understand more clearly. I also acknowledge that I may have contributed to some of her pain through my ignorance and intolerance. When she and I talk, we discuss the millions of other young Black men and women who face similar obstacles and do not have the positive familial support she does. Some are cut off from their families, run out of their schools and neighborhoods, are bullied, raped, and even murdered. We critique our community for creating false dichotomies and double standards. Think about it: A murdering drug dealer can be forgiven for his sins, do his time, and come home to his old neighborhood—oftentimes with great fanfare. But if a man chooses to love another man, he is treated like a pariah and condemned to hell. For Black males to inhabit a healthy mental state, we must adopt a language of tolerance and acceptance of others, despite all the social messages we receive to the contrary.

Nobody ever taught us that sexuality exists on a continuum ranging from heterosexual to homosexual, with many nuances in between. The responsibility to address homophobia and create safe spaces for all people to develop a healthy sexual identity is not the sole responsibility of gay, bisexual, transgender, and queer brothers. We must encourage our brothers who are in the process of discovering and expressing their sexuality to seek allies who can support them, whether in a community group, a church, a birth family, or a supportive nonbirth family.

Either consciously or unconsciously, many Black males believe the stereotype that we are hypersexed "brutes," as if it is our job to conquer as much sex as possible. The only caveat is that it must be with a woman—anything else is blasphemy. Most Black men treat someone whose sexual practices fall outside the heterosexual norm with hostility, fear, and sometimes violence. This often results in men either leading a double life (sometimes called "the down low") or suppressing their emotions, which can lead to substance abuse or suicide. With fear, intolerance, and lack of understanding for Black men, *among Black men*, the vicious cycle continues.

To encourage healthy lifestyles among Black males, it is our duty to allow one another to become our most complete and full selves, whatever our sexual orientation. In order to create sustainable change it is ultimately the responsibility of straight men to use our voices, our power, and our privilege to fight for the rights of us all.

KEYS TO MENTAL HEALTH

My mentor once told me, "The key to mental health for Black men is to always have options. And one is always better than none. As long as we have an option, we can create a pathway; because without them we are trapped, and nothing good comes from being trapped."

That conversation stuck with me and I've applied it to my life and my work with Black males. For us as Black men and Black boys to move toward mental wellness, we must create safe spaces where we can begin to deconstruct our lives and identify our mental health needs. To address collective healing and liberation, it is imperative to create communities and networks of nurturing, support, empowerment, and accountability. It is futile to employ a "don't ask, don't tell" policy with our loved ones in the hope that they can "suck it up" and "be all right." In addition to treating symptoms, we must employ strategies to correct social, political, and economic structures that continue to disenfranchise Black people globally.

The most important part of that strategy is to identify mentors with whom Black males can talk openly and freely. We must create open and honest relationships to develop coping strategies and learn how to maintain healthy lifestyles. Because of the stigma regarding mental illness in the Black community, it is imperative that we begin to break the silence and break the mental chains that limit our psychological freedom.

One simple exercise would be for a man to tell a friend or family member of an experience that impacted his mental wellnesss—for better or for worse. After sharing, ask the person if they have ever witnessed or experienced a similar situation. Continue this dialogue and include other men in the discussion. Always remember that we are our best resource.

When we see our brothers struggling, we need to throw out a lifeline. It is during these critical times that people begin to self-medicate with food, drugs, alcohol, sex, and other risky behaviors. Once out of desperate states, we then face the challenge of negotiating the consequences of our actions. Unfortunately, the costs of our actions are typically more severe and lasting than the original pain. Positive choices bring positive results, and the reverse is also true.

As Black males become more comfortable with the language of mental health, we must be ruthlessly honest with ourselves so that we know when we need to seek help. A web of support is crucial to maintaining mental health, because it can be difficult to realize that help is needed unless there is a monitoring system in place. There is no need to suffer when help is available from mental health care professionals, spiritual leaders, friends, colleagues, and family. Seeking support and discussing problems means that you are a survivor. Remember ours is not the story of a victim, but, rather the tale of a conqueror.

Strategies for Maintaining Mental Wellness

1. *Create communities of support.* In order to address our urgent need for collective healing and liberation, we need to build our own networks of nurturing support.

2. *Raise your critical consciousness.* Develop a heightened sense of awareness about how race, class, gender, sexual orientation, and educational status impact you on an individual, familial, and community level. Use this understanding to transform yourself and the systems in which you are embedded.

3. *Be proactive and address your own issues related to anger and temper.* If you find that you shut down or become explosive when you are sad, hurt, or enraged, you may want to seek individual, family, or group counseling to "unpack" and work through those feelings and get to the root of the problem. Typically, it is not the most recent event that you are reacting to, but some other unresolved pain or

trauma that a particular person or situation reminds you of.

4. *Educate yourself about mental wellness.* Being proactive and seeking information about mental
health will help you make informed choices about
your lifestyle.

5. *Get professional help.* Seek out mental health professionals who are trained to address your unique
mental health needs. When seeking a consultation,
do not minimize your symptoms. Share your process with a family member or friend.

6. *Take a position of nonviolence in every aspect of your
life.* Begin to examine past experiences of violence as
both a victim and a perpetrator. Seek support and
healing from the pain and take accountability for
things you may have done to others.

7. *Talk about your feelings.* Sharing your feelings
with others and being listened to can help enor-
mously.

8. *Maintain a healthy and active lifestyle.* Physical activity is a proven way to maintain mental wellness.

9. *Eat well.* A balanced diet is essential to maintaining
good mental health.

10. *Detox from drugs and alcohol.* Eliminating drugs
and alcohol from your life enables you to gain a
sense of clarity and become more connected to
thoughts and feelings that may be suppressed by
these substances. This will also enable you to assess
for addictions. If you are addicted to a substance, it
will be extremely difficult to stop, and you may
need to seek additional support.

11. *Drink sensibly.* Even though it can make you feel good in the short term, alcohol is a depressant. If you must drink, do so in moderation, particularly when you are feeling low or anxious.

12. *Keep in touch with friends and loved ones.* Close relationships have a huge impact on how we feel on a daily basis so manage them as best you can. If you do not have friends or family, seek people who can support you through groups and organizations, religious institutions, and other networks.

13. *Learn how to handle stress.* Develop better coping skills and relaxation techniques. Take breaks and vacations. A change of scenery can change the way we feel about things.

14. *Do something you are good at.* Activities can distract you from negative feelings and promote a sense of well-being through achievement.

15. *Accept who you are.* Acknowledging our good and bad points can help us to see things in perspective. It can also help us set realistic expectations of ourselves, play to our strengths, and accept the things we cannot do.

16. *Care and advocate for others.* Helping others can make you feel useful and needed. It also creates opportunities to improve the communities we live in. In order to change our mental health, we must change the conditions that influence our wellness.

17. *Connect to your spiritual core.* It is necessary to be centered physically, mentally, emotionally, and spiritually. Critically examine your belief systems and find a place of worship or meditation that affirms your humanity.

7

Ending Violence Against Women and Girls

By Kevin Powell

In my recent travels and political and community work and speeches around the country, it became so very obvious that many American males are unaware of the monumental problem of domestic violence in our nation. This seems as good a time as any to address this urgent and overlooked issue. Why is it that so few of us actually think about violence against women and girls, or think that it's our problem? Why do we go on believing it's all good, even as our sisters, our mothers, and our daughters suffer, and a growing number of us participate in the brutality of berating, beating, or killing our female counterparts?

All you have to do is scan the local newspapers or ask the right questions of your circle of friends, neighbors, or co-workers on a regular basis, and you'll see and hear similar stories coming up again and again. There's the horribly tragic case of Megan

Williams, a twenty-year-old West Virginia woman, who was kidnapped for several days. The woman's captors forced her to eat rat droppings, choked her with a cable, and stabbed her in the leg while calling her, a Black female, a racial slur, according to criminal complaints. They also poured hot water over her, made her drink from a toilet, and beat and sexually assaulted her during a span of about a week, the documents say. There's the woman I knew in Atlanta, Georgia, whose enraged husband pummeled her at home, stalked her at work, and finally, in a fit of fury, stabbed her to death as her six-year-old son watched in horror. There's the woman from Minnesota, who showed up at a national male conference I organized a few months back with her two sons. She had heard about the conference through the media, and was essentially using the conference as a safe space away from her husband of fifteen years who, she said, savagely assaulted her throughout the entire marriage. The beatings, both in front of her two boys and when she was alone with her husband, were so bad she said, that she had come to believe it was just a matter of time before her husband would end her life. She came to the conference out of desperation, because she felt all her pleas for help had fallen on deaf ears. There's my friend from Brooklyn, New York, who knew, even as a little boy, that his father was hurting his mother, but the grim reality of the situation did not hit home for him until, while playing in a courtyard beneath his housing development, he saw his mother thrown from their apartment window by his father. There's my other friend from Indiana who grew up watching his father viciously kick his mother with his work boots, time and again, all the while angrily proclaiming that he was the man of the house, and that she needed to obey his orders.

Perhaps the most traumatic tale for me these past few years was the vile murder of Shani Baraka and her partner, Rayshon

Holmes, in the summer of 2003. Shani, the daughter of eminent Newark, New Jersey, poets and activists Amiri and Amina Baraka, had been living with her oldest sister, Wanda Pasha, part-time. Wanda was married to a man who was mad abusive—he was foul, vicious, dangerous. And it should be added that this man was a "community organizer." Wanda tried, on a number of occasions, to get away from him. She called the police several times, sought protection and a restraining order. But even after Wanda's husband had finally moved out, and after a restraining order was in place, he came back to terrorize his wife—twice. One time he threatened to kill her. Another time he tried to demolish the pool in the backyard, and Wanda's car. The Baraka parents were understandably worried. Their oldest daughter was living as a victim of perpetual domestic violence, and their youngest daughter, a teacher, a girls' basketball coach, and a role model for scores of inner-city youth, was living under the same roof. Shani was warned, several times, to pack up her belongings and get away from that situation. Finally, Shani and Rayshon went, one sweltering August day, to retrieve the remainder of Shani's possessions. Shani's oldest sister was out of town, and it remains unclear, even now, if the estranged husband had already been there at his former home, forcibly, or if he had arrived after Shani and Rayshon. No matter. This much is true: he hated his wife Wanda and he hated Shani for being Wanda's sister, and he hated Shani and Rayshon for being two women in love, for being lesbians. His revolver blew Shani away immediately. Dead. Next, there was an apparent struggle between Rayshon and this man. She was battered and bruised, then blown away as well. Gone. Just like that. Because I have known the Baraka family for years, this double murder was especially difficult to handle. It was the saddest funeral I have ever attended in my life. Two tiny women in two tiny caskets. I howled so hard and long that I doubled over in pain in the church pew and nearly fell to the floor beneath the pew in front of me.

Violence against women and girls knows no race, no color, no class background, no religion. It may be the husband or the fiancé, the grandfather or the father, the boyfriend or the lover, the son or the nephew, the neighbor or the co-worker. I cannot begin to tell you how many women—from preteens to senior citizens and multiple ages in between—have told me of their battering at the hands of a male, usually someone they knew very well, or what is commonly referred to as an "intimate partner." Why have these women and girls shared these experiences with me, a man? I feel it is because, through the years, I have been brutally honest, in my writings and speeches and workshops, in admitting that the sort of abusive male they are describing, the type of man they are fleeing, the kind of man they've been getting those restraining orders against—was once *me*. Between the years 1987 and 1991, I was a very different kind of person, a very different kind of male. During that time frame I assaulted and/or threatened four different young women. I was one of those typical American males: hypermasculine, overly competitive, and drenched in the belief system that I could talk to women any way I felt, treat women any way I felt, with no repercussions whatsoever. As I sought therapy during and especially after that period, I came to realize that I and other males in this country treated women and girls in this dehumanizing way because somewhere along our journey we were told we could. It may have been in our households; it may have been on our block or in our neighborhoods; it may have been the numerous times these actions were reinforced for us in our favorite music, our favorite television programs, or our favorite films.

All these years later I feel, very strongly, that violence against women and girls is not going to end until we men and boys become active participants in the fight against such behavior. I recall those early years of feeling clueless when confronted—by both women and men—about my actions. This past life was brought back to me very recently when I met with a political associate who reminded me that he was, then and now, close friends with the last woman I assaulted. We, this political associate and I, had a very long and emotionally charged conversation about my past, about what I had done to his friend. We both had watery eyes by the time we were finished talking. It hurt me that this woman remains wounded by what I did in 1991, in spite of the fact that she accepted an apology from me around the year 2000. I left that meeting with pangs of guilt, and a deep sadness about the woman with whom I had lived for about a year.

Later that day, a few very close female friends reminded me of the work that some of us men had done, to begin to reconfigure how we define manhood, how some of us have been helping in the fight to end violence against women and girls. And those conversations led me to put on paper *The Seven Steps for Ending Violence Against Women and Girls*. These are the rules that I have followed for myself, and that I have shared with men and boys throughout America since the early 1990s:

1. *Own the fact that you have made a very serious mistake*, that you've committed an offense, whatever it is, against a woman or a girl. Denial, passing blame, and not taking full responsibility, is simply not acceptable.

2. *Get help as quickly as you can in the form of counseling or therapy* for your violent behavior. YOU must be willing to take this very necessary step. If you don't know where to turn for help, I advise visiting the website www.men stoppingviolence.org, operated by an important organization based in Atlanta that can give you a starting point

and some suggestions. Also visit www.usdoj.gov/ovw/ pledge.htm, where you can find helpful information on what men and boys can do to get help for themselves. Get your hands on and watch Aishah Shahidah Simmons's critically important documentary film *NO!* as soon as you are able. You can order it at www.notherape documentary.org. *NO!* is, specifically, about the history of rape and sexual assault in Black America, but that film has made its way around the globe and from that very specific narrative comes some very hard and real truths about male violence against females that is universal, that applies to us all, regardless of our race or culture. Also get a copy of Byron Hurt's *Beyond Beats and Rhymes*, perhaps the most important documentary film ever made about the relationship between American popular culture and American manhood. Don't just watch these films, watch them with other men, and watch them with an eye toward critical thinking, healing, and growth, even if they make you angry or very uncomfortable. And although it may be difficult and painful, you must be willing to dig into your past, into the family and environment you've come from, to begin to understand the root causes of your violent behavior. For me that meant acknowledging the fact that, beginning in the home with my young single mother, and continuing through what I encountered on the streets or navigated in the parks and the schoolyards, was the attitude that violence was how every single conflict should be dealt with. More often than not, this violence was tied to a false sense of power, of being in control. Of course the opposite is the reality: violence toward women has everything to do with powerlessness and being completely out of control. Also, we need to be clear that some men simply *hate* or have a very low regard for women and girls. Some of us, like me, were the victims of physical, emotional, and verbal abuse at the hands of mothers who had been completely dissed by our fathers, so we caught the brunt of our mothers' hurt and anger. Some of us were abandoned by our mothers. Some of us were sexually assaulted by our mothers or other women in our lives as boys. Some of us watched our fathers or other men terrorize our mothers, batter our mothers, abuse our mothers, and we simply grew up thinking that that male-female dynamic was the norm. Whatever the case may be, part of that "getting help" must involve the word *forgiveness*. Forgiveness of ourselves for our inhuman behavioral patterns and attitudes, and forgiveness of any female who we feel has wronged us at some point in our lives. Yes, my mother did hurt me as a child but as an adult I had to realize I was acting out that hurt with the women I was encountering. I had to forgive my mother, over a period of time, with the help of counseling and a heavy dose of soul-searching to understand who she was, as well as the world that created her. And I had to acknowledge that one woman's actions should not justify a lifetime of backward and destructive reactions to women and girls. And, most importantly, we must have the courage to apologize to any female we have wronged. Ask for her forgiveness, and accept the fact that she may not be open to your apology. That is her right.

3. *Learn to listen to the voices of women and girls.* And once we learn how to listen, we must truly *hear* their concerns, their hopes, and their fears. Given that America was founded on sexism—on the belief system of male dominance and privilege—as much as it was founded on the

belief systems of racism and classism, all of us are raised and socialized to believe that women and girls are unequal to men and boys, that they are nothing more than mothers, lovers, of sexual objects, that it is okay to call them names, to touch them without their permission, to be violent toward them physically, emotionally, spiritually—or all of the above. This mind-set, unfortunately, is reinforced in much of our educational curriculum, from preschool right through college, through the popular culture we digest every single day in music, sports, books, films, and the Internet, and through our male peers who often do not know any better, either—because they had not learned to listen to women's voices, either. For me that meant owning up to the fact that throughout my years of college, for example, I never read more than a book or two by women writers. Or that I never really paid attention to the stories of the women in my family, in my community, to female friends, colleagues, and lovers who, unbeknownst to me, had been the victims of violence at some point in their lives. So when I began to listen to and absorb the voices, the stories, and the ideas of women like Pearl Cleage, Gloria Steinem, bell hooks, Alice Walker, of the housekeeper, of the hair stylist, of the receptionist, of the school crossing guard, of the nurse's aide, and many others, it was nothing short of liberating to me. Terribly difficult for me as a man, yes, because it was forcing me to rethink everything I once believed. But I really had no other choice but to listen if I was serious about healing. And if I was serious about my own personal growth. It all begins with a very simple question we males should ask each and every woman in our lives: Have you ever been physically abused or battered by a man?

4. *To paraphrase Gandhi, make a conscious decision to be the change we need to see.* Question where and how you've received your definitions of manhood to this point. This is not easy as a man in a male-dominated society because it means you have to question every single privilege men have vis-à-vis women. It means that you might have to give up something or some things that have historically benefited you because of your gender. And people who are privileged, who are in positions of power, are seldom willing to give up that privilege or power. But we must, because the alternative is to continue to hear stories of women and girls being beaten, raped, or murdered by some male in their environment, be it the college campus, the inner city, the church, or corporate America. And we men and boys need to come to a realization that sexism—the belief that women and girls are inferior to men and boys, that this really is a man's world and the female is just here to serve our needs regardless of how we treat them—is as destructive to ourselves as it is to women and girls. As I've said in many speeches through the years, even if you are not the kind of man who would ever yell at a woman, curse at a woman, touch a woman in a public or private space without her permission, hit or beat a woman, much less kill a woman—you are just as guilty if you see other men and boys doing these things and you say or do nothing to stop them.

5. *Become a consistent and reliable male ally to women and girls.* More of us men and boys need to take public stands in opposition to violence against women and girls. That means we cannot be afraid to be the only male speaking out against such an injustice. It also means that no matter what kind of male you are, working-class or middle-class

or super-wealthy, no matter what race, no matter what educational background, and so on, you can begin to use language that supports and affirms the lives and humanity of women and girls. You can actually be friends with females, and not merely view them as sexual partners to be conquered. Stop saying "boys will be boys" when you see male children fighting or being aggressive or acting up. Do not sexually harass women you work with and then try to brush it off if a woman challenges you on the harassment. If you can't get over a breakup, get counseling. As a male ally, help women friends leave bad or abusive relationships. Do not criticize economically independent women because this independence helps free them in many cases from staying in abusive situations. Donate money, food, or clothing to battered women's shelters or other women's causes. Do not ever respond to a female friend with "Oh you're just an angry woman." This diminishes the real criticisms women may have about their male partners. American male voices I greatly admire, who also put forth suggestions for what we men and boys can do to be allies to women and girls, include Michael Kimmel, Jackson Katz, Charles Knight, Mark Anthony Neal, Jelani Cobb, Charlie Braxton, and Byron Hurt. Of course standing up for anything carries risks. You may—as I have—find things that you say and do taken out of context, misunderstood or misinterpreted, maligned and attacked, dismissed, or just outright ignored. But you have to do it anyway because you never know how the essay or book you've written, the speech or workshop you've led, or just the one-on-one conversations you've had, might impact the life of someone who's struggling for help. I will give two examples: A few years back, after giving a lecture at an elite East Coast college, I noticed a young woman milling about as I was signing books and shaking hands. I could see that she wanted to talk with me, but I had no idea of the gravity of her situation. Once the room had virtually cleared out, this seventeen-year-old first-year student proceeded to tell me that her pastor had been having sex with her since the time she was four, and had been physically and emotionally violent toward her on a number of occasions. Suffice to say, I was floored. This young woman was badly in need of help. I quickly alerted school administrators, who pledged to assist her, and I followed up to make sure that they did. But what if I had not made a conscious decision to talk about sexism and violence against women and girls, in every single speech I gave—regardless of the topic? This young woman might not have felt comfortable enough to open up to me about such a deeply personal pain. My other example involves a young male to whom I have been a mentor for the past few years. He is incredibly brilliant and talented, but, like me, comes from a dysfunctional home, has had serious anger issues, and, also like me, has had to work through painful feelings of abandonment as a result of his absent father. This, unfortunately, is a perfect recipe for disaster in a relationship with a woman. True to form, this young man was going through turbulent times with a woman he both loved and resented. His relationship with the young woman may have been the first time in his twenty-something years that he'd ever felt deep affection for another being. But he felt resentment because he could not stomach—despite his declarations otherwise—the fact that this woman had the audacity to challenge him about his anger, his attitude, and his behavior toward her. So she left him, cut him off, and he confessed to me that he wanted to hit her. In his mind, she was dissin' him. I was honestly stunned because I thought I knew this young man fairly well, but here he was, feeling completely powerless while thoughts of committing violence against this woman bombarded his mind and spirit. We had a long conversation, over the course of a few days, and, thank God, he eventually accepted the fact that his relationship with this woman was over. He also began to seek help for his anger, his feelings of abandonment, and all the long-repressed childhood hurts that had nothing to do with this woman, but everything to do with how he had treated her. But what if he had not had somebody to turn to when he needed help? What if he'd become yet another man lurking at his ex's job or place of residence, who saw in his ability to terrorize that woman some twisted form of power?

6. *Challenge other males about their physical, emotional, and spiritual violence toward women and girls.* Again, this is not a popular thing to do, especially when so many men and boys do not even believe that there is a gender violence problem in America. But challenge we must when we hear about abusive or destructive behavior being committed by our friends or peers. I have to say I really respect the aforementioned political associate who looked me straight in the eyes, sixteen long years after I pushed his close female friend and my ex-girlfriend into a bathroom door, and asked me *why* I had done what I did, and, essentially, *why* he should work with me all those years later. American males don't often have these kinds of difficult but necessary conversations with each other. But

his point was that he needed to understand what had happened, what work I had done to prevent that kind of behavior from happening again, and why I had committed such an act in the first place. Just for the record: no, it has not happened since, and no, it never will again. But I respect the fact that, in spite of my being very honest about past behavior, women and men and girls and boys of diverse backgrounds have felt compelled to ask hard questions, to challenge me after hearing me speak, after reading one of my essays about sexism and redefining American manhood. We *must* ask and answer some hard questions. This also means that we need to challenge those men—as I was forced to do twice in the past week— who bring up the fact that some males are the victims of domestic violence at the hands of females. While this may be true in a few cases (and I do know some men who have been attacked or beaten by women), there is not even a remote comparison between the number of women who are battered and murdered on a daily, weekly, monthly, or yearly basis in America and the number of men who suffer the same fate at the hands of women. Second, we men need to understand that we cannot just use our maleness to switch the dialogue away from the very real concerns of women to what men are suffering, or what we perceive men to be suffering. That's what step number three in the seven steps to ending violence against women and girls is all about. So many of us American males have such a distorted definition of manhood that we don't even have the basic respect to *listen* to women's voices when they talk about violence and abuse, without becoming uncomfortable, without becoming defensive, without feeling the need to bring the conversation, the dialogue, to us and our needs and our concerns, as if the needs and concerns of women and girls do not matter.

7. *Create a new kind of man, a new kind of boy.* Violence against women and girls will never end if we males continue to live according to definitions of self that are rooted in violence, domination, and sexism. I have been saying for the past few years that more American males have got to make a conscious decision to redefine who we are, to look ourselves in the mirror and ask where we got these definitions of manhood and masculinity, to which we cling so tightly. Whom do these definitions benefit and whom do they hurt? Who said manhood has to be connected to violence, competition, ego, and the inability to express ourselves? And while we're asking questions, we need to thoroughly question the heroes we worship, too. How can we continue to salute Bill Clinton as a great president yet never ask why he has never taken full ownership for the numerous sexual indiscretions he has committed during his long marriage to Senator Hillary Clinton? How can we in the hiphop nation continue to blindly idolize Tupac Shakur (whom I interviewed numerous times while working at *Vibe,* and whom I loved like a brother) but never question how he could celebrate women in songs like "Keep Ya Head Up" and "Dear Mama" on the one hand, but completely denigrate women in songs like "Wonda Y They Call U Bitch" on the other? What I am saying is that as we examine and struggle to redefine ourselves as men, we also have to make a commitment to questioning the manifestations of sexism all around us. If we fail to do so, if we do not begin to ask males, on a regular basis, why we refer to women and girls

with despicable words, why we talk about women and girls as if they are nothing more than playthings, why we think it's cool to "slap a woman around," why we don't think the rape, torture, and kidnap of Megan Williams in West Virginia should matter to us as much as the Jena 6 case in Louisiana, then the beginning of the end of violence against women and girls will be a long time coming.

8

I Am A Man

By William Jelani Cobb, Ph.D.

*When men can no longer love women they also cease to respect
or trust each other, which makes their isolation complete.
Nothing is more dangerous than this isolation, for men will
commit any crimes whatever rather than endure it.*

—James Baldwin

I am a man. My nephew's eyes plead this statement—even as
they betray his confusion over the word's precise meaning. We
are cold, on the side of a mountain in January, trying to get to the
bottom of some things. He wears a thin blue excuse for a jacket
that matches his jeans and cap, and keeps his words as sparse as
the growth on this barren stretch. I walk him off the road, farther
and farther into the recesses of this mountain until it seems we
are only pursuing more cold. Twenty-four hours earlier I was
home in Atlanta teaching the history of the Civil War, then my
sister called, pleading with me to save her son's life. And now, a
plane, a Greyhound, and a car ride later, I am in rural Pennsyl-
vania stamping my feet against the cold and walking farther into
the brittle brush of this mountain trying to get to a deep, stark
place with my twenty-year-old namesake.

When we find a clearing I take a seat on top of a rock and we begin to exchange words. He admits to hitting his girlfriend, the mother of a boy who carries his name and therefore mine. His thin frame corroborates his mother's story, that he has been drinking to excess and becoming increasingly erratic and violent in his behavior, sinking into a pattern that we know well from our personal history. We are all heirs to the failed experiments in manhood that stand like bitter monuments in our family history. She called me because she fears for his life and because I am the only male in my immediate family who has managed to avoid substance abuse and incarceration and she thinks that I can share the key to that riddle with her son because this is why she named him after me.

I am a man.

This is the most complex, the most audacious and misunderstood statement in our culture. Black men, since the shackled beginnings of our history in this country, have whispered it to ourselves until we believed it, or at least came closer to believing it. You can say it aloud for a century and you will only begin to see how deep this goes. Making this affirmation—*I am a man*—and understanding it has been one of our central struggles in the four centuries of history we have accrued on these shores. This is what I spoke to my nephew about on that rock in January—the history that preceded us, and the history that lives inside us, and how we cannot move forward until we understand and confront all of that.

Even under the best of circumstances, it is no simple task for any of us to come to an understanding of who we are and our relationship to the world. But Black males in this country were plagued from the very outset by a set of contradictions that warp identity into a riddle that each of us, whether we wish to admit it or not, spends a great deal of our lives trying to solve. What exactly does it mean to be a Black man? This vexing question is the natural result of living in a society where it was required that you grow older without growing up, where the ideals of "manhood" are to protect and provide but both law and custom prevent you from doing either, where violence and domination are the cornerstones of manhood, but you are the target of violence and under the legal control of other men.

The American concept of "manhood" was largely a mix of secondhand European sexism and the roughhouse gunslinger values honed on the frontier. We know, or ought to know by now, that a great deal of American history has been devoted to ensuring that the words "Black man" is a contradiction in terms. The consequence is that for Black males the ideals of "manhood" are like a receding shoreline that becomes more distant with the passing years—leaving us further and further adrift. The poet Elizabeth Alexander once asked a roomful of brothers how many of us were *free* men. The fact that each of us had to think about the question was all the answer she needed.

Even a one-eyed glance reveals that a disproportionate amount of Black culture is concerned with the question of manhood. The early Black abolitionists adopted the motto "Am I Not a Man and a Brother?" and two centuries later their civil rights movement descendants carried banners and signs that shouted the words "I Am a Man" to the world. We see that same fixation in the folklore that came out of slavery: it inhabits the blues, it was layered inside the elegant sentences of James Baldwin, and it is the reason Richard Wright wrote *Native Son* with enough force to give the reader a concussion. We cannot hope to understand the culture of hiphop without understanding the fractured, fragile history of Black boys and Black men in this country. The attempt to declare one's manhood to the world is the common theme beneath nearly every boast, every metaphor, every rhyming jewel dropped since the culture began. The reason for this is clear: we only protect that which has value and that which we fear can be taken from us.

Emancipation delivered Black people into a kind of dazed semi-freedom after the Civil War but it also inspired the brutes of the Old South to new levels of madness. The result of their attempts to resurrect slavery was the organized terrorism of lynching, festivals of murder that claimed the lives of some three thousand Black men during the late nineteenth and early twentieth centuries. From Georgia we have this report from 1899:

> Sam Hose shrieked at the sight of the knife and quietly urged his tormentors to kill him swiftly. This was a plea none was inclined to heed ... The torture of the victim lasted almost half an hour. It began when a man stepped forward and very matter-of-factly sliced off his ears. Then several men grabbed Hose's arms and held them forward so his fingers could be severed one by one and shown to the crowd. Finally a blade was passed between his thighs, Hose cried in agony, and a moment later his genitals were held aloft. Three men lifted a large can of kerosene and dumped its contents over Sam Hose's head, and the pyre was set ablaze.

This ritual of death was repeated at a rate of nearly twice per week in the South for almost thirty years. White mobs targeted Black families, and specifically Black males for these public murders, using castration as a means of denying the very manhood—as it is understood in the most barbaric terms—of Black men. Denying this unspeakable assault and the toll it exacted from us has been at the heart of Black male culture ever since.

It is no coincidence that at the very point in history where Black men were being set on fire and castrated for recreation,

Black culture created the myth of Stag-o-Lee, the violent, invulnerable Black bad man who was immune to danger and endowed with superheroic sexual abilities.

There were two sides of this coin: On the one hand these tales served as a kind of coping mechanism, a means of insulating oneself from the brutality of the outside world. It required a certain kind of audacity to create these tales of powerful Black men in a society where Black men were designated as exactly the opposite.

But the other side of the coin was that Black manhood came to embrace the twisted ideals of masculine domination that existed in broader America. It is not coincidental, for instance, that during the same time period when Black women were being portrayed as sexually immoral and loose by the white public, we began to see these same statements echoed by Black men. In 1901, William Hannibal Thomas, a Black man, wrote a book called *The American Negro: What He Was, What He Is, and What He May Become*, in which he declared that Black women and their sexual immorality—not Jim Crow, not segregation, not lynching—were the primary reason the Black race had not advanced.

We can trace the descent of these ideas—the virtues of violence and the contempt for Black women—through distinct generations and histories and witness them combining with racism and economic exploitation to create the barriers that now stand between us as brothers, husbands, fathers, friends, and members of our communities. They are the very reason why we pause when asked the question *Are you a free man?*

We inherit these insecurities from the Black males who preceded us, and bequeath them to those who come after. And it is not difficult to see where this has gotten us. We live in a world where Black men are nineteen times more likely than Whites to be murdered, and where young Black women are more likely than their White counterparts to experience violence at the hands of the men in their lives. We see 68 percent of our children born to single-parent households, which in itself would not be such a damning reality if such a high percentage of black fathers did not disappear entirely from the lives of their children.

I spoke to my nephew on that cold mountain about the blind alleys we have walked down, the fragile, halfhearted, incomplete brand of manhood that was birthed in this experience. I told him that we have embraced the brute's version of manhood for which the highest virtue is to instill fear in the hearts of others in order to camouflage our own.

But I did not leave him with that.

We also have a parallel tradition, one in which generations of Black males have struggled and given life to a fuller version of ourselves. None of us is flawless, none without contradictions, but many of us are accomplished and have laid out a more human path for us to walk.

There is a long lineage of Black men who understood violence not simply as a means of dominating others, but as a last-ditch tactic to be used in defense of their loved ones, even in the midst of slavery. One unnamed slave attacked and beat an overseer who attempted to beat his wife and was forced to flee into the woods, where he lived for eleven months.

In the midst of slavery and the attempts to destroy the Black family, Black men went to great lengths to preserve their familial bonds. From Louisiana we have the report of George Sally, an enslaved Black man who disobeyed the White slaveholder and left the plantation to visit his wife. When he was arrested and thrown into prison for disobedience he stated that he would gladly do the same again if it meant seeing his wife.

Another Black man walked nearly twelve hours every Sunday in order to spend a few hours with his wife on a distant plantation, only to have to turn around and walk home in time to begin the next day's work. The history of the South is littered with reports of Black males who, after the end of slavery, set out on foot to find the wives and children they had been sold away from. Historical accounts of these "wanderers" testify that these men covered thousands of miles, cutting paths across the South, moving from town to town and from farm to farm to keep their family ties alive.

One slave who had learned to write before he was sold away wrote a letter to his wife, saying:

> I am sold to a man by the name of Peterson in New Orleans . . . give my love to my mother and father and tell them "Goodbye" for me, and if we shall not meet in this world I hope we meet in heaven. My dear wife for you and my Children I cannot express the [grief] I feel to be parted from you . . . I remain your truly husband until Death.

Another slave's letter laments the separation that came when he was sold away from his family, then selflessly accepts the tragic reality that they cannot be together. He wrote begging his wife to find "a good, smart man" to marry and to please send him some of his children's hair.

While confused men like William Hannibal Thomas sought to trample the reputation of Black women, Frederick Douglass demanded that women be given the right to vote and wrote that "the woman has the right to equal liberty with the man." W. E. B. Du Bois was not only a brilliant critic of racism and White supremacy, he also recognized the dead end that sexism and violence would lead us to. He argued that the burden of Black women had to be carried by Black men as well, writing, "To no modern race does its women mean so much as to the Negro, nor come so near to the fulfillment of its meaning." Looking at the conditions of rape and sexual coercion that confronted Black women, Du Bois said:

> I shall forgive the South much in its final judgment day; I shall forgive slavery for slavery is a world-old habit, I shall forgive its fighting for a well lost cause and for remembering that struggle with tender tears . . . but one thing I shall never forgive, neither in this world nor the world to come: its wanton and continued insulting of the Black womanhood which it sought and seeks to prostitute to its lust.

Huey P. Newton, founder of the Black Panther Party, urged African Americans to recognize that sexism and homophobia were obstacles to our own freedom. Bayard Rustin, a Black gay man who organized the 1963 March on Washington, wrote that Black people could never achieve our full civil rights as long as Black women were denied their equal rights.

At our best, most honest moments, we have used hiphop not as a means of disguising our humanity behind boasts and bling, but as a place to honestly examine what it means to be a man. This is the space Tupac inhabited when his pen produced "Brenda's Got a Baby," and what De La Soul touched upon when they wrote sympathetically about a sexually exploited young woman in "Millie Pulled a Pistol on Santa."

I spent three hours that night in the woods speaking to my nephew about the ways in which we find ourselves trapped in a world not of our own making, acting out a script written by brutes and handed to us like leftovers fed to slaves. We hope to understand that those words, *I am a man*, carry weight, that they obligate you to walk twelve hours for your woman and to make a point that an evil world cannot kill your capacity to love. It means that we would rather spend eleven months in the woods than see one of our sisters harmed.

I told my nephew that I am a student and teacher of history and that I know the obstacles that stand behind us are larger than those that stand in front of us. Bitter and painful history has led us into this situation, but the solutions we seek and the examples we need also lie in this history. So this is the task, to mine our souls for those jewels that will sustain us, and leave the rest to pass into dust.

Who's Who in
The Black Male Handbook

Kevin Powell (Editor and Contributor) is a poet, essayist, hiphop historian, public speaker, entrepreneur, and political activist. A product of extreme poverty, welfare, and a single-mother-led household, Kevin is a native of Jersey City, New Jersey, and was educated at both Rutgers University and Pace University, where he received an honorary doctorate. He is a longtime resident of Brooklyn, New York, and it is from his base there that Kevin has authored or edited nine books, including his two most recent, *No Sleep Till Brooklyn*, a collection of poetry (Soft Skull Press, 2008), and *The Black Male Handbook*. Indeed, Kevin does extensive work around American and African American male development. That work includes lectures, workshops, and writings on the necessity of redefining manhood away from male domination, sexism, violence, and homophobia. Kevin is a part of the United Nations secretary-general's Unite to End Violence Against Women campaign across the globe, and is working closely with Amnesty International to prevent violence against girls in schools in America and abroad. Kevin has been a Writing Fellow for the

Joint Center for Political and Economic Studies, as well as a Phelps Stokes Fund Senior Fellow. His literary output has appeared in numerous publications through the years, among them *Esquire,* the *Washington Post, Essence, Rolling Stone,* and *Vibe.* At *Vibe,* Kevin was a founding staff member and served as a senior writer where he profiled iconic figures such as General Colin Powell, and where he became the definitive documentarian on the life and times of the late Tupac Shakur. Kevin's life is dedicated to public service, and his organizational affiliations include Moveon.org, the NAACP, the Sierra Club, and Alpha Phi Alpha Fraternity, Inc. He can be emailed at kevin@kevinpowell.net.

Hill Harper (Foreword Writer) is author of the bestseller *Letters to a Young Brother* (Gotham Books, 2006), which won two NAACP awards and was named Best Book for Young Adults by the American Library Association in 2007. Currently starring in *CSI: NY,* playing Dr. Hawkes, a role for which he won the 2008 Image Award for Outstanding Actor in a drama series, Hill has appeared in numerous prime-time television shows and feature films, including *The Sopranos, ER, Lackawanna Blues, He Got Game, The Skulls, In Too Deep, The Nephew,* and *The Visit.* Hill graduated magna cum laude with a B.A. from Brown University (and was valedictorian of his department) and cum laude with a J.D. from Harvard Law School. He also holds a master's degree with honors from Harvard's Kennedy School of Government. He is a motivational speaker around the country. Named one of *People's* Sexiest Men Alive, he lives in Los Angeles. You can contact Hill via www.manifestyourdestiny.org.

Lasana Omar Hotep (Contributor) is an educator, consultant, and entrepreneur committed to inciting critical thought about society, culture, and politics. He has spent over eighteen years working toward the cause of creating harmonious human relationships. Hotep is a native of Los Angeles, came of age in San Antonio, Texas, and currently resides in Phoenix, Arizona. He has served as a collegiate student leader at Texas State University, a grassroots community organizer, and a member of several advisory boards. Hotep has contributed chapters to several publications, including *African-American Men in College* (Jossey-Bass, 2006), *The State of Black Arizona* (ASU, 2008) and *Be a Father to Your Child* (Soft Skull, 2008). Hotep developed the African American Men of Arizona State University (AAMASU) Program. AAMASU is both a college organization and a high school readiness program serving Black males and their families. Nationally, Lasana serves as a member of the Student African American Brotherhood (SAAB) faculty. Lasana is the founder, principal owner, and lead consultant of Hotep Consultants. He also serves as a student success coordinator in the Multicultural Student Center at Arizona State University. Lasana is a member of Alpha Phi Alpha Fraternity, Inc. Hotep can be reached at lasana @lasana hotep.com.

Jeff Johnson (Contributor) serves as a trusted voice for information and opinions to a new generation. A social activist, political strategist, inspirational speaker, executive producer, and architect for social change, Johnson is one of today's most gifted leaders in both the political and entertainment arenas. Johnson has spent the last decade carving out a unique niche that merges the worlds of politics and popular culture to provide cutting-edge strategic and leadership-based consulting for youth and urban demographics. Of paramount importance to Johnson is his political and social activism, comprising roles as the national youth director for the NAACP and vice president of Russell Simmons's Hip Hop Summit Action Network. An established journalist, he has interviewed such marquee figures as 2008 presidential candidates Barack Obama and Hillary Clinton, as well as the Honorable Minister Louis Farrakhan. Jeff is one of only two news correspondents to interview Sudan's president Omar Al-Bashir within the past thirteen years, and he is the only American reporter to receive an exclusive interview with Africa's first female head of state, Ellen Johnson-Sirleaf, in Liberia. Johnson provides commentary in leading urban lifestyle magazines and serves as an international correspondent for various news outlets. Johnson may be emailed at jeffjohnson@ascendantstrategy.net.

Byron Hurt (Contributor) is an award-winning documentary filmmaker, a published writer, and an antisexist activist. His most recent documentary, *Hip-Hop: Beyond Beats and Rhymes* premiered at the Sundance Film Festival and was broadcast nationally on the Emmy Award–winning PBS series *Independent Lens*, drawing an audience of 1.3 million viewers. *Chicago Tribune* named *Hip-Hop: Beyond Beats and Rhymes* "one of the best documentary films in 2007." Hurt also directed and produced *I AM A MAN: Black Masculinity in America*, a sixty-minute award-winning documentary that captures the thoughts and feelings of African American men and women from over fifteen cities across America, and challenges audiences to examine the damaging effects of patriarchy, racism, and sexism in American culture. Hurt is a former Northeastern University football quarterback and a gender violence prevention educator. He is a founding member of the Mentors in Violence Prevention (MVP) program, the leading college-based rape and domestic violence prevention initiative for college and professional athletics. Over the last fifteen years, Hurt has lectured at hundreds of campuses, presented at numerous professional conferences, and trained thousands of young men and women on issues related to gender, race, sex, violence, music, and visual media. A member of Omega Psi Phi Fraternity, Inc., Byron Hurt can be emailed at info@bhurt.com.

Ryan Mack (Contributor), president of Optimum Capital Management, has a life mission to build and develop a durable financial empire geared toward educating his community and beyond. He charitably lends his support to corporations, inner-city communities, and international communities by coordinating workshops teaching the principles of understanding the power of financial planning. Fortune 500 companies, unions, churches, government-subsidized housing communities, municipal programs, nonprofits, international communities, gang members, youth, and colleges and universities have benefited from the financial classes and workshops that he has developed and instructed through Optimum Capital Management. He has been profiled in Tavis Smiley's *Covenant and Action*, featured in *Black Enterprise* magazine, and received Tom Joyner's "Hardest Working Financial Advisor Award" because of his efforts to empower the community with the crucial life skills of financial literacy. Ryan's organization memberships include the Optimum Institute of Economic Empowerment, Inc. (president and founder), All About Business (president and founder), and Alpha Phi Alpha Fraternity, Inc. Mr. Mack can be emailed at info@optimum-capital.com and his company website can be viewed at www.optimum-capital.com.

Kendrick B. Nathaniel (Contributor) is a seasoned mentor/life coach, youth advocate, community actionist, entrepreneur, security consultant, and heavily certified fitness professional. The product of a single-parent household, Kendrick credits his mother, Eliza, with his tenacious desire to leave his community and his world a whole lot better than he found it. Kendrick's tireless passion as a mentor/life coach fuels his constant participation in all things that nurture tomorrow. As a youth advocate, he lends his experience, time, and talent to various youth initiatives throughout the country to assist, encourage, and assure young people that they are the future and that they can and will make contributions to society—contributions, indeed, that reach far beyond their wildest dreams. Kendrick currently serves as the executive director of A.U.N.T. & U.N.C.L.E. Youth Employment Service, Inc., a not-for-profit organization unconditionally vested in the efforts to break the cycle of socialized poverty by providing assistance to underserved youth to harness their potential to be productive members of their community as well as society. After more than fifteen years as a certified fitness pro, Kendrick is counted among the best in the industry, in the greater New York area. A native New Yorker, Kendrick was raised in Walterboro, South Carolina, and educated at Central Texas College and Norfolk State University. He is a veteran of the United States Navy, SPECWAR. He can be emailed at Kendrick@KBernardConsortium.net.

Andraé L. Brown, Ph.D. (Contributor) is a graduate of Elizabeth City State University, earned his master's in education in school counseling at the University of Maryland Eastern Shore and his Ph.D. in marriage and family at Seton Hall University. Brown is an assistant professor at Hunter College–CUNY. His research interests include developing treatment models that use families, schools, and communities to address trauma, violence, and substance abuse, and examining resilience in street-life-oriented Black men. As co-director of Affinity Counseling Group, he provides clinical services, organizational consultations, workshops, and trainings that focus on shifting mental health paradigms from pathology to health and liberation, community building, and social justice initiatives. Brown is a fellow of the Council for Contemporary Families and proud member of Omega Psi Phi

Fraternity, Inc. Dr. Brown can be reached at ABro@hunter.cuny
.edu and Affinitygrp@optonline.net.

William Jelani Cobb, Ph.D. (Contributor), is a father, a friend, an
uncle, and associate professor of history at Spelman College. He
specializes in post–Civil War African American history, twentieth-
century American politics, and the history of the Cold War. He is
a contributing writer for *Essence* magazine, and an essayist and
fiction writer. Jelani is the author of *To the Break of Dawn: A Free-
style on the Hip Hop Aesthetic* (NYU Press, 2007), as well as *The
Devil & Dave Chappelle and Other Essays* (Thunder's Mouth,
2007). He is also editor of *The Essential Harold Cruse: A Reader.*
Born and raised in Queens, New York, he was educated at Jamaica
High School, Howard University in Washington, D.C., and Rutgers University where he received his doctorate in American history. He is a recipient of the Fulbright Fellowship and his reviews
and essays have appeared in the *Washington Post, Emerge*, the *Progressive*, the *Washington City Paper, ONE Magazine*, and Alternet
.org. Jelani has contributed to a number of anthologies including
In Defense of Mumia, Testimony, Mending the World, and *Beats,
Rhymes and Life*. He has also been a featured commentator on
National Public Radio and a number of other national broadcast
outlets. Jelani can be reached at www.jelanicobb.com.

Michael Scott Jones (Photographer) is an accomplished photographer specializing in entertainment, beauty and glamour, commercial, and fine-art photography. Michael has shot dozens of
CD covers and artists including Mary J. Blige, Willie Nelson, John
Legend, Tori Amos, LL Cool J, and 3 Doors Down, to name a few.
Michael's photos have been published in several magazines, including *Vibe, Essence, XXL*, and *Bleu*. Authors whom Michael has
shot include Kevin Powell, Quincy Troupe, Toni Blackman, and

Terrance Dean. In addition to *The Black Male Handbook*, Michael has shot Black males as the official photographer for the Black and Male in America town hall meetings, the State of Black Men ten-city national tour, and April Silver and Kevin Powell's "Hip-Hop Speaks" community series. Michael Scott Jones has been a multimedia producer since 1989, when he co-founded Nia Software. Michael was hired in 1999 by HBO to help develop an urban Internet portal for the hiphop generation through AOL/Time Warner's *Volume.com*. As the director of entertainment and multimedia, Michael produced multimedia projects for Internet, television, and film. Michael is currently the director of multimedia for Interactive One, a Radio One company, where he is responsible for photography, video, and audio for online properties including News One, Giantmag.com, the Urban Daily, and Hello Beautiful. For more about Michael Scott Jones's photography visit www.msjimages.com.

Kerry DeBruce (Graphic Designer) launched KLAD Creative, a full-service design firm in New York, eight years ago with her first clients: Sony Records, VP Records, Cicatelli Associates Inc., and Planned Parenthood of Nassau County. Armed with a bachelor's of arts in design from the esteemed Cooper Union for the Advancement of Science and Art, Kerry has received awards from both the Art Director's Club and AIGA. With over ten years of experience as a graphic designer and art director, her professional background includes positions at major advertising agencies, design houses, and the Metropolitan Museum of Art. However, much of Kerry's work in the entertainment industry spiraled from her experience working at Loud Records/Sony Music. In the last eight years, KLAD Creative's attention to detail and unique ability to capture the essence of their clients one pixel at a time has led to contracts with major entertainment industry companies, and KLAD is on the speed dial of every in-house art director and urban savvy marketing company. With Kerry DeBruce at the helm, KLAD Creative is a one-stop creative shop. She is also a fine artist, interior designer, event planner, and craft specialist. You can reach Kerry at kerry@kladcreative.com or by visiting her website, www.kladcreative.com.

Derek Felton (Contributor) is a speaker, coach, and agent of personal change. He has engaged more than twenty-thousand students and professionals throughout the United States with his philosophies on attitude, self-confidence, and living a life of purpose. His first book, *Brilliance Is Your Birthright: 12 Steps to Fulfilling Your Potential and Living Your Purpose*, was released in the summer of 2008. Derek is also the publisher of www.motivated brothas.com, a personal development site for Black men worldwide. A graduate of Chicago State University, he currently lives in Harlem, New York. To book Derek for a keynote presentation or workshop visit www.derekfelton.com.

Sidik Fofana (Researcher) is a writer, poet, and teacher. Hailing from the inner city of Boston, Sidik graduated from Columbia University in 2005 with a B.A. in English and anthropology. Since graduation, he has focused his writing on hiphop and cultural politics. Sidik's work has appeared in several publications such as the *Source*, okayplayer.com, and *Bounce*. He currently serves as associate editor at www.allhiphop.com and most recently wrote Erykah Badu's career publicity bio for her album *New Amerykah*. Sidik's short stories have been published on www.newyorkreview .org and he has recited poetry at the storied Nuyorican Poets Cafe. Sidik has also done volunteer work with the Harlem Book Fair, the Black Writers Conference, and the Black and Male in America three-day national conference. He currently lives in Harlem and teaches at a high school in Brooklyn. Sidik can be reached at sidik@allhiphop.com.

Geneva S. Thomas (Kevin Powell's research assistant) is an artist-scholar and native of Detroit. She holds an interdisciplinary B.A. in history, theater, and Black diasporic studies from Michigan State University, where she studied Black women's language, feminism(s), and performance. Geneva has studied throughout Africa, the Caribbean, and Europe. As a graduate student at New York University, her current interests deal with representations of Black women's bodies in fashion and the body politic. Geneva is currently hard at work developing "The Black Girl[Politic]" a body installation and discourse that addresses the complicated the politics of Black female dress and citizenship. She lives in Brooklyn and can be emailed at geneva.s.thomas@gmail.com.

APPENDIX

Nine Things You Can Do to Improve Yourself and Help Others

Compiled by Kevin Powell and April R. Silver

1. Seek God. When we seek God we are seeking the highest level of knowledge. Respect the presence and contributions of those who've come before us. The greatest "thank you" we could give to whatever God(s) we believe in, and to those people who've come before us, is to make a serious commitment to our personal and collective well-being, growth, and empowerment.

2. Read read read. Seek out reading lists, ask folks for book suggestions. Read at least one daily paper and one weekly alternative newspaper regularly. You must see reading as a commitment to learning. This will help broaden your worldview and sharpen your critical thinking skills. With this in mind, minimize television watching, or, at least, balance television viewing with reading, as constant reading will help you to interpret *all* media, including television, in a broader and healthier way.

3. Strive to be of good character, learn to be compassionate toward the plights of others, and struggle for consistency between your public and private lives. Always be conscious of what you say, think before you speak, and ask yourself, "Am I about bridge building or destroying bridges?" or "Do I know how to love myself, and others?"

4. Be proactive with your life and in your community. For example, educate yourself about the history of voting in America, register to vote, and vote in each and every election. Voting does make a difference on the local and state levels, as evidenced by who gets to control our school systems, land usage, and monetary allotments to our communities. Finally, join an organization that is in support of average, everyday people. Develop a high threshold for the difficulties associated with organization building, and with various personalities. If one organization disappoints you, seek out others, or make it a point to learn how to build an organization yourself by studying various groups and movements, then start one with like-minded folks.

5. Debate ideas and learn to formulate your own opinions. Debate in a healthy manner: always come with facts, not emotionalism, and make sure you are listening as opposed to waiting for your turn to speak. In other words, use your intellect, not your ego.

6. Avoid frivolous spending at all costs. Purchase what you need, not what you desire. Strive to own something in your life, be it a home, a business, or land.

7. Make a commitment to holistic living: eat healthy, exercise regularly, pray or meditate at least once every day, and seek out counseling in one form or another if you have *any* minor or major emotional issues.

8. Be creative. Discover what your creative expression is (e.g., writing, dancing, sewing, cooking, playing music). Learn the political and cultural history of your people, your group, and other people, other groups, so that you can develop a global vision.

9. Be bold, be fearless. We should never be afraid of living our lives with a commitment to honesty. And we must be comfortable with resisting and protesting when necessary.

Recommended Readings

Visions for Black Men, by Na'im Akbar

I Know Why the Caged Bird Sings, by Maya Angelou

The N Word: Who Can Say it, Who Shouldn't, and Why, by Jabari Asim

The Fire Next Time, by James Baldwin

The Black Woman: An Anthology, edited by Toni Cade Bambara

Blues People, by Amiri Baraka (LeRoi Jones)

Before the Mayflower: A History of Black America, by Lerone Bennett

Smart Money Moves for African-Americans, by Kelvin Boston

Beyond the Down Low: Sex, Lies, and Denial in Black America, by Keith Boykin

Getting Good Loving: Seven Ways to Find Love and Make It Last, by Audrey B. Chapman

Deals with the Devil: And Other Reasons to Riot, by Pearl Cleage

The Death of Rhythm and Blues, by Nelson George

The Autobiography of Malcolm X, with Alex Haley

Letters to a Young Brother, by Hill Harper

Standing in the Shadows: Understanding and Overcoming Depression in Black Men, by John Head

Recommended Readings

Rock My Soul: Black People and Self-Esteem, by bell hooks

We Real Cool: Black Men and Masculinity, by bell hooks

Their Eyes Were Watching God, by Zora Neale Hurston

Soledad Brother, by George Jackson

Post Traumatic Slave Syndrome: America's Legacy of Enduring Injury and Healing, by Dr. Joy Degruy Leary

Why Should White Guys Have All the Fun? How Reginald Lewis Created a Billion-Dollar Business Empire, by Reginald F. Lewis and Blair S. Walker

The Bluest Eye, by Toni Morrison

The Women of Brewster Place, by Gloria Naylor

Who's Gonna Take the Weight? Manhood, Race, and Power in America, by Kevin Powell

Let's Get Real: Exercise Your Right to a Healthy Body, by Donna Richardson

I Will Survive: The African American Guide to Healing from Sexual Assault and Abuse, by Lori S. Robinson

Fast Food Nation, by Eric Schlosser

For Colored Girls Who Have Considered Suicide When the Rainbow Is Enuf, a choreopoem/play by Ntozake Shange

Be a Father to Your Child: Real Talk from Black Men on Family, Love, and Fatherhood, edited by April R. Silver

The Healing Wisdom of Africa, by Malidoma Patrice Some

All About Love: Favorite Selections from In the Spirit on Living Fearlessly, by Susan L. Taylor

Rap Attack 3, by David Toop

Acts of Faith: Daily Meditations for People of Color, by Iyania Vanzant

Core Performance: The Revolutionary Workout Program to Transform Your Body and Your Life, by Mark Verstegen

The Color Purple, by Alice Walker

Recommended Readings

Being a Black Man: At the Corner of Progress and Peril, by the staff of the *Washington Post*

White Like Me, by Tim Wise

The End of America: Letter of Warning to a Young Patriot, by Naomi Wolf

Black Boy, by Richard Wright

A People's History of the United States, by Howard Zinn

Welcome to the Terrordome: The Pain, Politics and Promise of Sports, by Dave Zirin

Note: These are suggestions. These volumes cover the areas of political, economic, cultural, spiritual, mental, and physical growth, development, and wellness. They all encourage progressive critical thinking and do-something-ism, and the titles represent both male and female voices.

Recommended Films
and Documentaries

A Raisin in the Sun (1961; directed by Daniel Petrie)

Antwone Fisher (2002; directed by Denzel Washington)

Bastards of the Party (2005; directed by Cle "Bone" Sloan)

Beah: A Black Woman Speaks (2003; directed by Lisa Gay Hamilton)

Beloved (1999; directed by Jonathan Demme)

Beyond Beats and Rhymes (2007; directed by Byron Hurt)

Billy Elliott (2000; directed by Stephen Daldry)

Blackout (2007; directed by Jerry LaMothe)

Bowling for Columbine (2002; directed by Michael Moore)

Boyz N the Hood (1991; directed by John Singleton)

Brother Outsider: The Life of Bayard Rustin (2003; directed by Nancy Kates and Bennet Singer)

Chisolm '72: Unbossed and Unbought (2004; directed by Shola Lynch)

Citizen King (2004; directed by Orlando Bagwell and W. Nolan Walker)

Claudine (1974; directed by John Berry)

Color Adjustment (1992; directed by Marlon Riggs)

Recommended Films and Documentaries

The Color Purple (1985; directed by Steven Spielberg)

Cooley High (1975; directed by Michael Schultz)

Daughters of the Dust (1991; directed by Julie Dash)

Do the Right Thing (1989; directed by Spike Lee)

The Education of Sonny Carson (1974; directed by Michael Campus)

Eve's Bayou (1997; directed by Kasi Lemmons)

Eyes on the Prize: Parts 1 & 2 (1987, 1990; directed by Henry Hampton)

Glory (1989; directed by Edward Zwick)

The Great Debaters (2007; directed by Denzel Washington)

Here I Stand (1999; the life of Paul Robeson; directed by St. Claire Bourne)

The Hip Hop Project (2006; directed by Matt Ruskin)

Hoop Dreams (1994; directed by Steve James)

Hotel Rwanda (2004; directed by Terry George)

Intimate Portrait: Harriet Tubman (2000; directed by Tiffany McLinn Lore and Suju Vijayan)

The Journey of the African-American Athlete (1996; directed by William C. Rhoden)

Killer of Sheep (1977; directed by Charles Burnett)

Life and Debt (2001; directed by Stephanie Black)

Life Is Beautiful (1997; directed by Roberto Benigni)

Lumumba (2000; directed by Raoul Peck)

Malcolm X (1992; directed by Spike Lee)

Meeting David Wilson (2008; directed by David A. Wilson and Daniel J. Woolsey)

NO! The Rape Documentary (2006; directed by Aishah Shahidah Simmons)

Nothing but a Man (1964; directed by Michael Roemer)

The Price of a Ticket (1990; life of James Baldwin; directed by Karen L. Thorson)

Recommended Films and Documentaries

The Rise and Fall of Jim Crow: Programs 1–4 (2002; directed by Bill Jersey and Richard Wormser)

Sankofa (1993; directed by Haile Gerima)

Sicko (2007; directed by Michael Moore)

Sounder (1972; directed by Martin Ritt)

Sunshine State (2002; directed by John Sayles)

Super Size Me (2004; directed by Morgan Spurlock)

Talk to Me (2007; directed by Kasi Lemmons)

To Kill a Mockingbird (1962; directed by Robert Mulligan)

Tongues United (1989; directed by Marlon Riggs)

Tupac: Resurrection (2003; directed by Lauren Lazin)

Whale Rider (2003; directed by Niki Caro)

What's Love Got to Do With It (1993; directed by Brian Gibson)

When We Were Kings (1996; directed by Leon Gast)

Y Tu Mamá También (2001; directed by Alfonso Cuarón)

Recommended Music CDs

Mama's Gun, Erykah Badu
Rapture, Anita Baker
Pet Sounds, The Beach Boys
Sgt. Pepper's Lonely Hearts Club Band, The Beatles
The Long Road to Freedom: An Anthology of Black Music, Harry
    Belafonte (producer)
My Life, Mary J. Blige
Star Time, James Brown
Buena Vista Social Club (soundtrack), Buena Vista Social Club
Patsy Cline Showcase, Patsy Cline
A Love Supreme, John Coltrane
Portrait of a Legend 1951–1964, Sam Cooke
Celia y Johnny, Celia Cruz and Johnny Pacheco
Kind of Blue, Miles Davis
Not a Pretty Girl, Ani DiFranco
The Chronic, Dr. Dre
Highway 61 Revisited, Bob Dylan
Ella Fitzgerald Sings the Duke Ellington Songbook, Ella Fitzgerald
    with the Duke Ellington Orchestra
Amazing Grace, Aretha Franklin

Recommended Music CDs

I Never Loved a Man the Way I Love You, Aretha Franklin

What's Going On, Marvin Gaye

Tanto Tempo, Bebel Gilberto

I'm Still in Love with You, Al Green

Are You Experienced?, The Jimi Hendrix Experience

The Miseducation of Lauryn Hill, Lauryn Hill

The Ultimate Collection, Billie Holiday

Rhythm Nation 1814, Janet Jackson

Off the Wall, Michael Jackson

At Last, Etta James

Surrealistic Pillow, Jefferson Airplane

Pearl, Janis Joplin

Tapestry, Carole King

All for You: A Dedication to the Nat King Cole Trio, Diana Krall

The Last Poets, The Last Poets

Princesses Nubiennes, Les Nubians

Abbey Is Blue, Abbey Lincoln

Ray of Light, Madonna

Mama Africa: The Very Best of Miriam Makeba, Miriam Makeba

Natural Mystic, Bob Marley

Blood on the Fields, Wynton Marsalis and the Lincoln Center Jazz
 Orchestra

Super Fly (soundtrack), Curtis Mayfield

Blue, Joni Mitchell

Nevermind, Nirvana

Sign O' the Times, Prince

It Takes a Nation of Millions to Hold Us Back, Public Enemy

The Dana Owens Album, Queen Latifah

Californication, Red Hot Chili Peppers

Promise, Sade

Anthology, Nina Simone

In the Wee Small Hours, Frank Sinatra

Recommended Music CDs

Club Classics Vol. I, Soul II Soul

Earth Crisis, Steel Pulse

Love. Angel. Music. Baby., Gwen Stefani

The Essential Barbra Streisand, Barbra Streisand

Live at Carnegie Hall, Sweet Honey in the Rock

The Supremes (box set), The Supremes

Emperors of Soul (box set), The Temptations

The Doors, The Doors

Makaveli: The 7 Day Theory, 2Pac

The Unforgettable Fire, U2

The Best of Luther Vandross . . . The Best of Love, Luther Vandross

Saturday Night Fever (soundtrack), various artists

Voices of the Civil Rights Movement: Black American Freedom Songs 1960–1966, various artists

Sarah Vaughan Sings George Gershwin, Sarah Vaughan

Amistad (soundtrack), John Williams (composer)

New Moon Daughter, Cassandra Wilson

Songs in the Key of Life, Stevie Wonder

The Iron Pot Cooker, Camille Yarbrough

Recommended Safe Spaces
for Black Males

Compiled by Sidik Fofana

The Library

Reading can be just as enjoyable as watching television or playing sports. At most local libraries—libraries are *free* public spaces—all you need is a valid address and you can start checking out books the same day. Even if you're in school, the library can supplement your education by offering books on African American culture and history that most traditional classrooms do not offer. Since many inner-city areas lack good bookstores, the library is sometimes the only place to find worthwhile literature. In addition to books, the library organizes great programs like arts and crafts, book clubs, and author readings. And it is really a great place just to sit quietly, and reflectively, where no one will bother you.

The Museum

Looking at great works of art is one of the most stimulating activities you can engage in. A trip to the museum can enlighten you in ways you never imagined. That's right: the visual arts will expand your imagination, make you think more critically, take you to new worlds and new adventures. For example, many writers, musicians, and actors visit the museum for ideas and inspiration. The next time you go, study the works of Romare Bearden, Kara Walker, Jean-Michel Basquiat, and other influential Black visual artists. Museums range from being free to costing very little for a visit. Be sure to read the fine print about admission, because some museums say the admission is a "suggested donation," which means you do not have to pay it.

The Park

Never underestimate the value of fresh air. Many people use the park as a tranquil oasis from the chaos of daily life. Though neighborhood parks are generally used to exercise, relax, and read in, nationally known parks, like Central Park in New York City, make wonderful mini-vacation spots. Moreover, the park is free, it allows you to connect with nature, and regular visits there will help you simplify your life and unclutter your mind.

The Gym

Working out is just as important as any mental or spiritual training. The gym offers an assortment of strength, calisthenic, and cardiovascular activities to ensure a well-rounded exercise regimen. According to the Prevention Center for Cardiovascular Disease, the average person should exercise for twenty to thirty minutes two to three times a week. The gym not only satisfies that recommendation, but it is also a nice place to network and make friends. But if you are into being in your own world there, all you have to do is plug into your iPod or the music or TV on one of the cardio machines and zone out. Prices vary for gym memberships, but the YMCA remains one of the best deals in America.

Hiking and Mountain Climbing

Experiencing the great outdoors is another rewarding activity. Mountain climbing is not as intimidating as it sounds, and expeditions are available at every skill level and location. As alternative lifestyles, hiking and mountain climbing can introduce adventure into your life. They can help you overcome fear, or the unwillingness to take walking seriously as an exercise (once you hike, you will understand why walking matters!).

Spiritual and Religious Institutions

In addition to being a place of prayer and worship, your church, mosque, synagogue, or temple is the positive link between you and your community. With programs such as retreats, fundraising dinners, and charity events, a religious institution can enrich you with social service projects. Meditating at home or practicing yoga at your local gym can also help you find that elusive peace of mind. There are many spiritual and/or religious institutions that are open all day every day, and are simply places where people come to pray, meditate, chant, be still, or do whatever they need to do. For example, there are many Buddhist temples that offer this. But you've got to be willing to explore what exists in your community. If you want peace of mind and a calm spirit, you've got to invest the time it takes to identify these kinds of spaces.

Recommended Safe Spaces for Black Males

Counseling and Therapy

Never be afraid to seek professional help or advice. Though the African American community has placed a heavy stigma on psychological medication and services, counseling is very essential to mental health. Even if you are not going through any stress or hardship, regular visits to a psychologist or psychiatrist can enhance your quality of life. Indulge in the opportunity to sit down and have a professional chat with your counselor for a couple of hours. And if you do not have medical insurance, be assertive and seek out free or low-cost counseling services in your community. They do exist.

Hobbies

Hobbies define who we are. How we spend our leisure is just as important as what we do during the workweek. Whether it's sports, music, or movies, hobbies bring recreation and purpose to your life. Yet, as African Americans, it is important for us to explore new pastimes as well. We can enjoy playing basketball and making music, but it's also beneficial to try activities out of our comfort zone. There is nothing wrong with feeding pigeons, stamp collecting, swimming, or taking free or low-cost classes in areas we know nothing about.

Creativity

Take every opportunity to nurture and expand your creativity. This can be as simple as keeping a journal or drawing in a sketchbook or taking photos on a regular basis. Your artistic contributions are essential especially in a world where our perspective is not always represented. Even if it's just a matter of documenting yourself in some form, creativity enables you to leave a piece of yourself for others to appreciate. And let's not limit creativity to the arts. It could include cooking, learning how to fix things in your home, or repairing an automobile—anything, really, that requires you to explore your inner genius outside of what you normally do from day to day.

Home (Wherever Home Is for You)

A home often reflects the character of the person who resides in it. Depending on how it is arranged and maintained, your home can have a positive or negative energy. It is an extension of you and can serve as a peaceful oasis from the grind of daily life. Keeping your home tidy and comfortable will keep your mind lighter and more relaxed. No matter what your status is economically, your home can be rich, vibrant, and a source of pride in your life.

Tips for Black Males
When Stopped by the Police

Compiled by the American Civil Liberties Union

To fight police abuse effectively you need to know your rights. There are some things you should do, some things you must do, and some things you cannot do. If you are in the middle of a police encounter, you need a handy and quick reference to remind you what your rights and obligations are.

Please visit www.aclu.org to get the following for *free*, as a download, so that you can carry it with you at all times.

THE BASICS, Part 1

1. Think carefully about your words, movement, body language, and emotions.
2. Don't get into an argument with the police.
3. Remember, anything you say or do can be used against you.
4. Keep your hands where the police can see them.
5. Don't run. Don't touch any police officer.
6. Don't resist even if you believe you are innocent.

7. Don't complain on the scene or tell the police they're wrong or that you're going to file a complaint.

8. Do not make any statements regarding the incident. Ask for a lawyer immediately upon your arrest.

9. Remember officers' badge and patrol car numbers.

10. Write down everything you remember ASAP.

11. Try to find witnesses and their names and phone numbers.

12. If you are injured, take photographs of the injuries as soon as possible, but make sure you seek medical attention first.

13. If you feel your rights have been violated, **file a written complaint** with the police department's internal affairs division or civilian complaint board.

THE BASICS, Part 2

1. What you say to the police is always important. What you say can be used against you, and it can give the police an excuse to arrest you, especially if you badmouth a police officer.

2. You must show your driver's license and registration when stopped in a car. Otherwise, you don't have to answer any questions if you are detained or arrested, with one important exception. The police may ask for your name if you have been properly detained, and you can be arrested in some states for refusing to give it. If you reasonably fear that

your name is incriminating, you can claim the right to remain silent, which may be a defense in case you are arrested anyway.

3. You don't have to consent to any search of yourself, your car, or your house. If you *do* consent to a search, it can affect your rights later in court. If the police say they have a search warrant, *ask to see it*.

4. Do not interfere with or obstruct the police—you can be arrested for it.

IF YOU ARE STOPPED FOR QUESTIONING

1. It's not a crime to refuse to answer questions, but refusing to answer can make the police suspicious about you. If you are asked to identify yourself, see paragraph 2 above.

2. Police may "pat down" your clothing if they suspect a concealed weapon. Don't physically resist, but make it clear that you don't consent to any further search.

3. Ask if you are under arrest. If you are, you have a right to know why.

4. Don't badmouth the police officer or run away, even if you believe what is happening is unreasonable. That could lead to your arrest.

IF YOU'RE STOPPED IN YOUR CAR

1. Upon request, show them your driver's license, registration, and proof of insurance. In certain cases,

your car can be searched without a warrant as long as the police have probable cause. To protect yourself later, you should make it clear that you do not consent to a search. It is not lawful for police to arrest you simply for refusing to consent to a search.

2. If you're given a ticket, you should sign it; otherwise you can be arrested. You can always fight the case in court later.

3. If you're suspected of drunken driving and refuse to take a blood, urine, or breath test, your driver's license may be suspended.

IF YOU'RE ARRESTED OR TAKEN TO A POLICE STATION

1. You have the right to remain silent and to talk to a lawyer before you talk to the police. Tell the police nothing except your name and address. Don't give any explanations, excuses, or stories. You can make your defense later, in court, based on what you and your lawyer decide is best.

2. Ask to see a lawyer immediately. If you can't pay for a lawyer, you have a right to a free one, and should ask the police how the lawyer can be contacted. Don't say anything without a lawyer.

3. Within a reasonable time after your arrest, or booking, you have the right to make a local phone call: to a lawyer, bail bondsman, a relative, or any other person. The police may not listen to the call to the lawyer.

4. Sometimes you can be released without bail or have bail lowered. Have your lawyer ask the judge about this possibility. You must be taken before the judge on the next court day after arrest.

5. Do not make any decisions about your case until you have talked with a lawyer.

IN YOUR HOME

1. If the police knock and ask to enter your home, you don't have to admit them unless they have a warrant signed by a judge.

2. However, in some emergency situations (such as when a person is screaming for help inside, or when the police are chasing someone) officers are allowed to enter and search your home without a warrant.

3. If you are arrested, the police can search you and the area close by. If you are in a building, "close by" usually means just the room you are in.

4. We all recognize the need for effective law enforcement, but we should also understand our own rights and responsibilities—especially in our relationships with the police. Everyone, including minors, has the right to courteous and respectful police treatment.

5. If your rights are violated, don't try to deal with the situation at the scene. You can discuss the matter with an attorney afterward or file a complaint with the internal affairs or civilian complaint board.

How to Take Care of and Present Yourself as a Black Male

Compiled by Derek Felton

NOTE: The tips in this section are not meant to be patronizing, but are here to give young Black males, especially, a step-by-step blueprint for life, reminders of the little things that many males of all races, classes, and backgrounds overlook in their daily lives.

I. Hygiene Tips for Black Males

Washing Your Hands

How often do you wash your hands or conduct breath checks throughout the day? As ragged as my father's hands could be after working on cars and driving trucks, I always saw him take care of them. Good personal hygiene is one of the most effective ways to keep you and others from getting sick. Germs are spread from person to person because we put our unwashed hands to our mouths.

Your hands should be rinsed with clean soap and water. Then dry them with clean paper towels. This is especially important if you've been playing with animals, using public transportation, shaking hands, drinking from a water fountain, or preparing food.

Taking Care of Bad Breath

Good dental hygiene includes regular brushing *and* flossing. Bad breath can be caused by diseases of the teeth and mouth or food stuck between gums. It's true that foods like garlic and onion are also culprits, but don't get it twisted. Not eating during the day can cause your breath to be tart as well. When you eat, your mouth produces saliva, which breaks down food and washes away bacteria. If you don't eat, Flaming Hot Cheetos won't be the only thing giving you the "dragon."

Mouthwashes, sprays, mints, and flavored chewing gum can make your breath smell better—but only temporarily. I'm not telling you to become a metrosexual and carry a "man bag." Still, it might be a good idea to keep hand sanitizer and a travel-size toothpaste and brush nearby for those times when your breath smells like you've got something on your mind.

Proper Showering and Bathing Techniques

Believe it or not, there are correct and incorrect ways to take showers and baths. Shower and bathe correctly and the healthier you'll be. They say cleanliness is next to godliness. Let's break down how to keep your temple spotless.

- Make sure that you undress completely before you get in the tub. You can't get completely dirt-free if you have on underwear or a T-shirt.
- Turn on the water to your preferred temperature. If you like it warmer, turn it up; if you like cold showers, lower the temperature. Get under the water and

get your entire body wet. Be sure to rinse your face as well.

- Take a clean washcloth and bar of soap and hold both under the water. It's best to use antibacterial soap to help kill more germs. Rub them both together to get a good amount of the soap onto the cloth.
- Scrub yourself all over with the washcloth. Don't forget to get behind your ears, back of your neck, your legs and feet, and in between each toe.
- Rinse off the soap and, if necessary, repeat each step.
- Get out of the shower. Standing on a rug or mat, gently dry your face, arms, hair, pelvic region, chest, back, legs, and feet.
- After you dry off, be sure to rub lotion on your entire body—not just your arms and legs. This will help prevent "ashiness" and cracked skin.
- *Important!* Apply deodorant generously to your whole armpit area as soon as you are dried off. This is going to help keep bacteria from forming and producing odor.

II. Dress and Style Tips for Black Males

Things to Know About Suits

There are many occasions—some unexpected—where you might need a suit. Weddings, funerals, interviews, and graduations are a few instances that come to mind. With that said, there are a few basics about suits that need to be addressed. If you can avoid it, do not wear odd-colored, pimped-out suits—unless you're going to the Players Ball, of course. The yellow suit with the black pin-stripes and extra-wide shoulders was acceptable in 1942, but if you wear it today, plan on getting some sideways stares.

Pick a neutral color that's versatile such as navy, black, gray, or brown. If you don't own a suit yet, just get a nice jet-black one made of quality lightweight wool that you can wear year round. Ask for help from someone more experienced who can assist you in finding the right garment.

This may seem obvious, but make sure your suit fits. If you buy a suit off the rack, you can be certain that it needs to be altered. Take your garment to a tailor who actually makes you put the suit on and takes your measurements. Don't have a tailor? No problem. Usually, a local dry cleaner offers this service at a very low price.

I understand that not everyone can afford $250–$600 suits. The good news is that you don't have to break yourself to look good. The department stores Marshalls and Filene's Basement have plenty of suits for $150. A store like K&G always has a "Buy two suits for $80" deal going on. If you can't swing that, go to the Salvation Army or a thrift store and grab one for $10. And many churches collect clothing from their members and give them away for free.

In the event that none of those are possibilities for you, just do the best you can with what you have. Always make sure that your white button-up dress shirt is clean, and you have a neat pair of slacks. The idea is to feel confident and be as presentable as possible no matter what you're wearing.

Shoes

Stay away from wearing brightly colored shoes in red, blue, or white. Your shoes should be made of leather; stick to lace-up or slip-on business shoes, preferably black or dark brown. Invest in a good pair; even if you don't wear them daily on the job, you'll need them for other occasions and you should expect to get a lot of years out of good shoes.

Make sure that your belt matches your shoes. If you are wearing black shoes, throw on a black belt. The same thing goes for brown belts and shoes.

A Final Word About Style

I've said this before and I'll say it again: just be clean, comfortable, and confident. There are some men who never wear suits and always dress down, such as entrepreneur Russell Simmons. He's someone I admire because he knows who he is and what works for him. It's not uncommon for him to wear a tuxedo with a pair of shell-toe Adidas. But he has a personal style that works for him because of the work he does and a certain level of success he's attained. Depending on who you are and what you're doing you may not be able to get away with that and that's fine—just be the best you that you can be.

Your personal style is evident in everything that you do— from the way that you dress to the things that you own. A sport coat hanging in your closet, the way you wear your Kangol, or the high-def television in your house . . . all of these choices represent your individual sense of what's pleasing and tasteful. Once you define your style, learn how to express it with confidence.

III. Etiquette Tips for Black Males

The Right Way to Shake Hands

Historically, handshakes were used to show the other person that you were unarmed. Today, we use it to greet people in all sorts of settings: business, church, the football field, and the workplace. But, like most things, there's a proper way to do it.

How to Take Care of and Present Yourself

Here are a few tips to help you get a "grip" on things:

1. While looking the person in the eye, extend your right hand with your thumb pointed at an upward angle to meet the other person's right hand. Never attempt to shake with your left hand.
2. Wrap your hand around the other person's when the loose skin between your index fingers and thumbs meet. This area is called the "web."
3. Grasp the hand firmly and squeeze gently. Limp handshakes are a big turnoff and make you appear weak. However, you also want to avoid a bone-crushing grasp that will make the other person squirming in pain.
4. Pump your hand up and down two or three times. Don't shake vigorously as if trying to mix a beverage!
5. It's common for men to have clammy hands, but no one wants a wet and nasty greeting. Quickly swipe your right hand on your pants, so that when you present it, it's dry.

Lastly, a good handshake says that you have your stuff together and can subconsciously influence others to do business with you.

Behavior with Women

One of the biggest complaints I hear from women is that men don't act like gentlemen anymore. They say that we don't open doors for them or offer our seats when they're standing. Then men say that they don't do it because women don't respect it and therefore don't deserve it. I say, brothers, just do it; just be a gentleman no matter what. You can't control what other people do, but you can control your behavior. Plus, it's the right thing to do. And when you're right, you can never be wrong.

Boy, Stand Up Straight!

A thing as simple as good posture can make you look taller and confident. Confident men are the ones who get the most attention and respect. When I was about twelve years old my uncle had me look in a mirror at how I was standing. He told me to lift my chin, not to crouch my shoulders, and to straighten my back. He was trying to help me visualize myself as being strong and healthy.

Good posture can help you stave off injury to your back, hips, and neck. It can also improve your concentration. By improving your posture you can instantly improve how you feel and you'll appear more attentive and competent. When you walk, stand, and sit bent over, people think you're a slouch.

Developing poor posture is like anything else that requires effort: difficult. Change takes willpower and it's always easier to do what we shouldn't. But good posture will increase your energy level, raise your self-esteem, and make you look better.

Being Humble Doesn't Mean You're Weak

Humility means being respectful and courteous toward others. It's not letting people walk all over you. You can display humility in social settings by saying "please" when asking for something and by saying "thank you" when it's given to you. These are simple courtesies that go a long way when dealing with people. Folks will know that you have manners and that you respect them.

Present-day hiphop makes such a big deal out of a man having *swagger*. I'm all for being secure and knowing who you are. But too much of it starts to turn into conceit, arrogance, and vanity—rarely do these qualities inspire admiration from your associates. You don't have to take a backseat and deny your self-worth. Being humble allows you to be aggressive in going after what you want, and lets others have their dignity, too.

IV. Grooming Tips for Black Males

Picking the Right Cologne

If you're like most people, your morning ritual probably includes brushing your teeth, washing your face, and taking a shower. But before you dry off and splash on an oh-so-fresh scent, there are a few things to consider.

Be sure that the fragrance you choose blends well with your natural scent. Not all aromas are created equal. Colognes react with your skin, and what smells like roses on you may smell like lemons on someone else. Therefore, not all fragrances will smell good on you. Ask your mom, sister, wife, girlfriend, or partner if they like the scent on you. Their feedback will help you make the right decision.

The fragrance should make you feel confident, but it should not announce your arrival five minutes before you enter a room (or require windows to be opened when you leave). Choose one that's fresh and light enough that only those who are standing close to you will notice.

Unless you want folks to run for cover, don't spray the cologne into all of your crevices in an attempt to create an invisible force field. And despite what your boys say, squirting a cloud of mist in the air and then standing under it is not a good idea. Fragrances are made to cling to your skin, not your clothes. Just put about a quarter of a teaspoon in your hand and apply to your neck. This should be enough to get you through the day.

How to Take Care of and Present Yourself

Keep Your Wig Tight

Don't you feel good when you look at yourself in the mirror while sitting in your barber's chair? Getting a fresh haircut is right up there with getting a crispy pair of Air Force 1's. You get compliments and even start walking with more of a swagger when you know your hair is tight. Not to mention the fact that others will respect you and take you more seriously because they'll know you take pride in your appearance.

If you haven't had a haircut in a while and don't know what to get, every barber has that big poster with all types of styles on it—from low Caesars and tapers to short Afros and twists. All you have to do is point and say, "Gimme number 7."

Barbers can be costly, and if you don't mind spending $15–$20 every week or so, then so be it. When I couldn't afford to peel off a "dub" I asked my friend to cut me up for $5. If you can't afford to spend money on haircuts every week, you might want to invest in a set of clippers and do it yourself.

A Few More Things

Fellas, please keep your fingernails clipped to a reasonable length and your lips moisturized. For example, if you go out to play basketball and there's a flicking sound when you shoot, your nails are way too long. You don't have to go to the nail salon, just keep some nail clippers available to chop your claws down. I recommend using a file to smooth out the rough edges and make the tip of the nail as round as possible.

For chapped lips you should always have Carmex, Chap Stick, or a lip balm containing petrolatum or beeswax. Dry lips can make it difficult to do everyday things like smiling, eating, or speaking. Sore and peeling lips can be caused by dehydration, cold air, and certain medications that treat acne. None of us are

LL Cool J so you'll also want to avoid licking your lips because the saliva will evaporate and leave your lips even drier.

V. Job Interview Tips for Black Males

You've been looking for a job for months now. Your résumé is posted on every website in cyberspace and you've given it to friends who promised to help you. Then you finally get a call from a human resources manager who wants to interview you—tomorrow. You're so excited that you could jump through the roof, but you don't know anything about the company or the responsibilities of your potential role.

You might have lots of experience or even an advanced degree. But if you don't walk into that interview poised, confident, and ready to seize the opportunity, you'll regret it. As dominant as Michael Jordan was on the hardwood, even he had to put in work.

Here are a few things you should always do to prepare for an interview:

- Prepare a list of questions to ask. The worst answer you can give a prospective employer to "Do you have any questions for me?" is "No." It makes you look disinterested and unprepared.
- Practice answering potential questions beforehand. Go over your responses to inquiries such as "What can you offer us that others can't?" "Why should I hire you instead of someone else?" and (this is my favorite) "Tell me about yourself."
- Make sure you get there on time! Arrive no more than fifteen minutes early. This shows that you're punctual and excited, but not overeager. It also ex-

hibits professionalism and gives you a minute to calm your nerves.

- Map out where you're going ahead of time. If you have a car or use public transportation, make sure you know exactly where it is in relation to where you live. If you have access to the Internet, use Google Maps. If you're driving and the interview location is not too far away, cruise by it beforehand. You don't want things like construction or making a wrong turn to cause you to be late.

- Always speak properly. I know that as Black males we live in two worlds and are fluent in at least two different languages: "ours" and "theirs." Even if the person interviewing you is a young brother who you think is cool, don't use street slang or hiphop lingo and steer clear of talking negatively about other races. His wife may be White and his best friend could be Asian—you never know. Another tip is to smile when you speak. It livens up the conversation and makes you appear bright and articulate.

How to Approach a Job Application

There will be times when you won't need a résumé and won't have a formal interview. However, most places will at least have you fill out an application to get a job. But you must know how to complete it accurately and neatly. So let's talk about how to correctly fill out an application.

- **Know your personal information.** Name, address, phone number, city, state, zip code. If you're not sure or have a "remembering problem," bring along a sheet of paper with the information already written on it.

- **Know what position you're applying for, when you can start, and how many hours per week you can work.** This is important because many employers base their hiring decisions on the applicant's availability and flexibility.

- **Know your previous employer's information.** All applications ask for this so you should have your former job's address, phone number, and supervisor's name. Put it on the sheet we talked about above.

- **Always write clearly using black or blue ink.** If the manager can't read your application and it looks like your six-year-old brother filled it out, it won't even be read. While we're on it, be sure to bring your own pen. How are you going to ask for a job and ask the employer for a pen?

- **Check for grammatical and spelling errors.** Please proofread your work before turning it in. A sloppy application with tons of misspellings casts doubt in an employer's mind about your intellect and attention to details. If you're not sure that it looks good, have someone else proofread your work.

Follow these steps and you'll increase your chances of finding work and moving up the ladder in your company.

LINK UP

For more resources for Black males, including organizations, toll-free hotlines, informational websites, models of success that you can duplicate in your city or town, employment, job training and small business options, prison reentry programs, and more, go to www.blackandmaleinamerica.org.

Acknowledgments

The Black Male Handbook was put together with great speed, and with a sense of urgency, given the times in which we live. To those points, I would like to thank a few key individuals to whom I am indebted for the publication of this book: first and foremost, Malaika Adero, my editor at Atria Books, for your vision and courage in agreeing to take this project on—*thank you very much;* Krishan Trotman, associate editor at Atria; Judith M. Curr, executive vice president and publisher, Atria Books; Kerry DeBruce, my graphic designer, and Michael Scott Jones, my photographer, whose collaboration created the great cover, and who have worked with me this entire decade on every single Black male initiative I've produced; Geneva Thomas, my incredibly brilliant and gifted assistant; Rob Kenner, my former editor at *Vibe*, one of the best editors in the literary world, period (thank you, Rob, for your eagle eye in looking over this manuscript several times); Sidik Fofana, who did the extensive research for this project; Derek Felton, who was gracious enough to compile, on short notice, all the great life skill tips at the back of this book; the American Civil Liberties Union, for always providing free and critical civil rights downloads and handouts for our nation; Nigel Radford, Diallo

Acknowledgments

Shabazz, and Jitu Weusi, our wonderful models for the cover; Hill Harper, my friend and colleague, for the terrific foreword; April Silver, my fellow activist and community organizer, with whom I've had the honor of working for two decades; all the writers who contributed to *The Black Male Handbook*—thank you very much for tolerating my editorial pressures (we got it done!); and to all the countless Black males, of all different backgrounds, whom I've met in my travels across America and overseas: I believe in all of you, and know that you all are the inspiration for *The Black Male Handbook*. In the words of the rapper Jadakiss:

We gon make it . . .